FATHOM

An Uncovering of Trauma

LISA DART

First published in 2019 by
Free Association Books

A CIP Catalogue of this book is available from the British Library

ISBN: 978-1-91138-328-4

Typeset by
Typo•glyphix
www.typoglyphix.co.uk

Cover design by
Candescent

Printed and bound in England

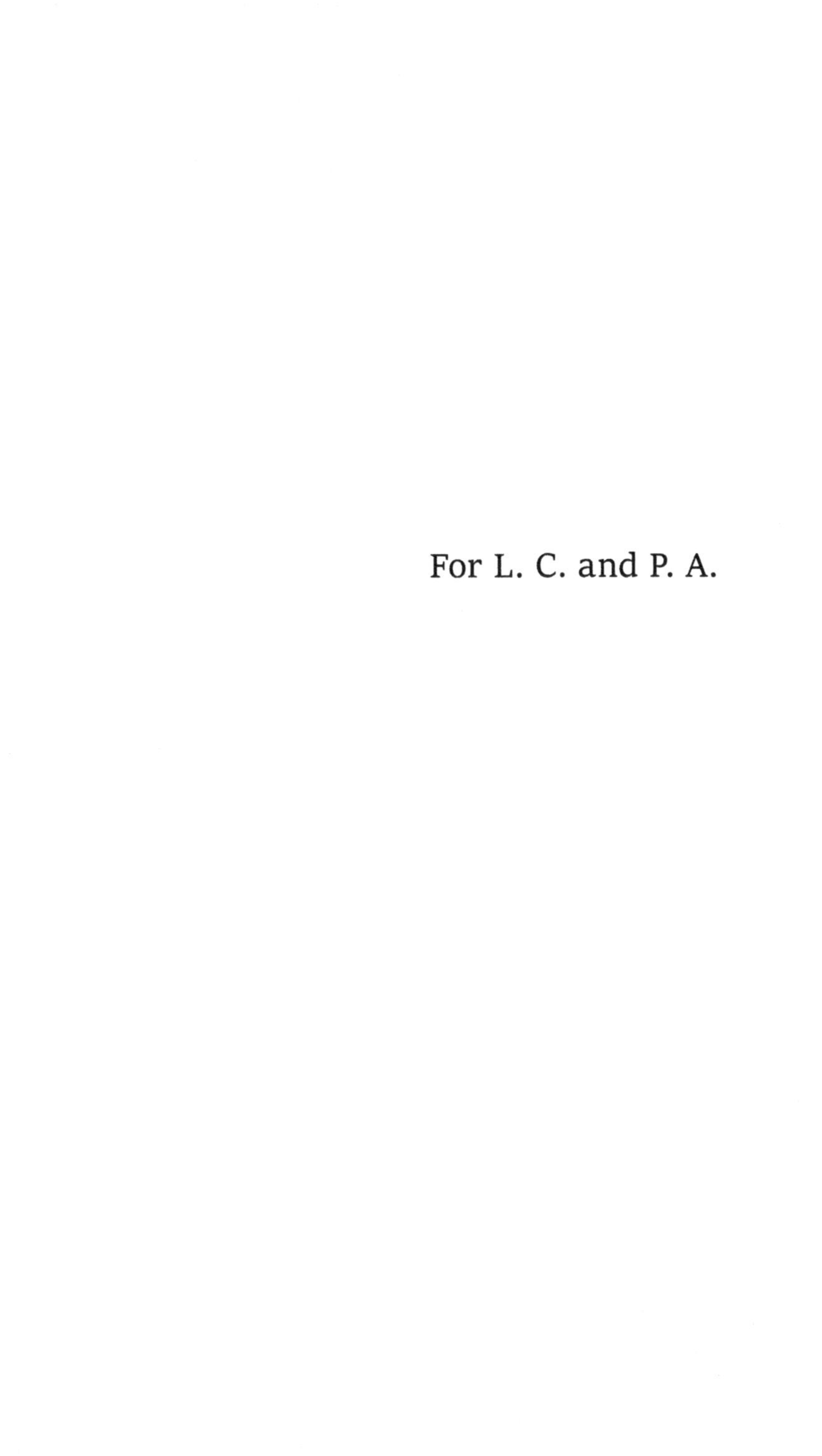

For L. C. and P. A.

Fathom

Oedipus: Hurl me into the sea where you can never look on me again.

Sophocles

Perhaps we find forgetfulness more of a riddle than memory today, now that a study of dreams and of pathological cases has shown that something we thought long forgotten can suddenly surface in the memory again.

Freud

1

Imagine.

It's 1965. England, south coast. Kent to be exact. My duffel coat is royal blue. And it is snowing. I am sitting on a chair in my next door neighbour's house. I am four years old. I like the word 'royal'. It makes the blue precise. Exact. Kingly, even. I will not leave the chair to play with my friend, my very best friend, and I will not take my coat off. I want to say, 'it is royal blue,' to show off that I know words like 'royal'. But I can't.

'Jenny's a funny girl,' my friend's mother tells my mother when she comes to fetch me. 'She wouldn't get down from the chair and she wouldn't take her coat off. She just sat there. Such a funny girl... fancy not wanting to play...'

This story has over the years folded itself into the fabric of my mind (my mother has repeated it many times) and I am fifty-two when I finally stretch the story out, smooth the creases, let it hang in the air in one long swathe. And I am, once again, sitting on a chair.

Not the chair against the yellow-framed French windows in my neighbour's house where I have my royal blue coat on. Nor is it against the black-framed windows in the house next door; (the semi-detached suburban house where I lived then, which is on the other side of the privet hedge at the front, on the other side of the wooden fence at the back, next to the fence the little stool my father made. My brother and sister stand on it to peer into my best friend's garden when I have been invited in to a party and they haven't.) No, the chair I am sitting on, after walking slowly up Brow Road – I am nearly always early these days – is brown leather, has a curved wooden frame and, when I sit, yields with a certain springiness. It dominates the small room.

Now another woman, my therapist, whom I shall call B, sits opposite me. She is talking to me as gently as anyone ever has. Even she has never talked this gently to me before:

Was it as if your friend's mother was saying to you, 'Well, would you like a sweet'?

And now, for a moment, B assumes a jauntiness as if she was my friend's mother all that time ago:

Perhaps she said: 'I'll get you a sweet. Then you can get down and go outside and play.'?

I shake my head.

B tries again:

Or 'Why don't you take your coat off then and come and play over here by the fire while I find you a sweetie?'

I ought to tell you B knows about me by now – what has happened to me but, as she says quite a lot at the beginning,

I can only know what you tell me...

So, you see, B can't mention the snow as I haven't told her that it was snowing. That all the trees outside are dark, the top of every branch perfect snow-ice. Nor that my cheeks and fingers are burning with the cold bite of the air. And I haven't told her my most recent dream of snow. Of the field and how the car's swerved tyre is a track on the white. Mud and water glimpsed through a sharp, glitter-cracked ice. Nor about the image I have saved on the computer of a white arcade of trees, the branches with the same skeletal dark, the exact same layering of snow. Perfect and complete. Nor of how the path vanishes, white, into the white horizon. And I haven't told her my memory of snow. Not because I am withholding – but because, because... because *the snow has no voice*. Yes, that's it – *the snow has no voice*. Nor have the garden's roses which, in my imagination, are ice-white. Speechless.

*

I have become best friends with the girl next door at number 6. She is pretty. I see her now with satin pink ballet shoes, with blunt block toes and a thin little bow at the front and white tights and, up her legs, long pink satin ribbons criss-crossed, and she is getting out of the wood-trimmed Morris Traveller onto the green verge and she has a hairband and her face is pale and her eyes are blue and there is a not-quite-sure-of-things look on her face I like (which she still has and I still like) and beyond the Morris Traveller over the road is the orchard and beyond that the primary school we will both go to in blue blazers and silver-striped ties and beyond that the collecting games we will play – beetles (in a Quality Street tin), car numbers (hiding them in the roof of her garage, classified), old spoons (silver dipped into thicketylicketylippety ice-cream), and beyond that the *yes* we will be given to sleep in a tent in her garden and the *yes* to stay up very late. And beyond that, high up on the hill, higher than the green playing fields, the girls' grammar school she will go to (all glass and flat front yellow panels) and it will be the year she is to take her O levels when she will be called into the headmistress's study and be asked about her mother who has the cancer that will kill her. She will be told, so nicely, 'You can always come to my study to talk or work quietly whenever you want to. Do you understand? Really, whenever ...'

And I will be on the swing going as high as I can whenever, whenever beyond and back, over the raspberry canes, beyond and back, beyond the orchard and the primary school and back, beyond the doe-brown eyes of Mrs Selwyn-Smith who stops me in the playground: 'How is your Daddy?'

And beyond the playground games, the boys flooding the girls' toilets and Jeannie Simmons crouching by the school boiler wetting herself three days in a row because she wears dresses with huge flowers in crinkly cotton in the winter, beyond the terror of the teacher with corn-coloured hair, red face and dry skin, and back, beyond the terror of the teacher, with a wrinkly, powdery, poker face and funny half-glasses... and far, far from the not knowing... the not knowing... the not knowing *times means multiply* (thwack three times on the desk with her long ruler) *times means multiply*... times means... and back, beyond the terror of... having the *for what we are about to receive may we be truly grateful* scoops of gravy with liver lumpies shiny black at the edges and... and... and in front of the class, sweaty hands slippy on a small round drum, stomach sick trying to get the time... and... and... my bs and ps and ss the wrong way round on pages and pages of strict feint lines... and back, and beyond the June-bloom roses and back, pulling harder and harder, faster and faster, beyond that long single scar of cloud, beyond everything that happened and had to be forgotten and into the sunlit air, higher and higher, into the reached-for summer-stretched and smoothed-out blue and yes, even higher and higher into what I will learn to say is the *infinite* though this word doesn't help me to know – I already know – I am one with it.

So many things I could say, but perhaps, because I am nervous, I repeat myself and say to my therapist:

Apparently, I do not move from my chair. My coat's buttoned up to the neck. Blue... my coat apparently (and now I hate that I am repeating the word 'apparently') *was royal blue.*

B makes another attempt, speaking to me very gently, but something in her usual tone started it all and something in the way her cheeks move even as she is speaking right now made me think of my next door neighbour, not my friend, but her mother. So I am thinking of the chair, my best friend's mother, the gardens, and my coat all at once in this story of myself. Something in the commonplace assurance, it will all be okay, really, everything will be okay, honestly it will, if you just have a sweetie and get down from the chair and go out into the garden and play. Somewhere there in B's parents-can-reassure-children-and-make-their-world-all-okay tone is my best friend's mother. Back then I am not convinced by anything. Not the promise of sweets, even though I think she has some of my favourite ones, black tubes of solid liquorice. Not the promise of the garden and the sun on the snow and all that good-for-me fresh air. Not the 'wouldn't you like to see if you can make a snowman?' Not even the anticipated joy of 'then I can tell your mummy what a good girl you've been.' Nothing will persuade me. I remain on the chair.

B's tone shifts now to the more inquiring one she has sometimes:

So where are your thoughts now?

It is her way of exploring the unspoken meanderings inside me:

... a large cherry blossom tree... slide... see-saw... sandpit... swimming pool... children laughing over the fence... my garden... holly trees... wooden arch... pear trees... rhubarb leaves... ragged raspberry canes... path petering out... my green swing, swinging... our lawn... roses... all round... roses...

Eventually I do say something else:

Back gardens... when I was a kid ...

*

In the work of analysis, there are stories; stories that rupture to redeem. But the beginnings of stories are elusive – as much as there are two gardens, there are two front rooms. The two front rooms are the same size. They have bay windows. My neighbour's, painted yellow. Ours, black. Black metal, although I have forgotten this.

(It is over forty years later when I see the black bay windows are replaced with new aluminium frames and whoever lives there has added a glass porch and there's an extension and a blue car in the drive, not my father's black Zephyr.)

Next door's back garden has a cherry blossom tree. I love the blossom and I like the branches and the leaves and the trunk, which is very thick. I like the bark too. I am seven years old. The branches stir in the wind. The blossom's pink. It petals both gardens. In my best friend's there's a blue and red climbing frame, a sandpit, swings and a small swimming pool. There is a coal bunker by the back door. At the front, the lawns of each house are separated by a privet hedge, a very thick green. One year, just before my family will move away, my friend and I help her father pull down the hedge. I remember the tussling of green, the light brown twisted woodiness underneath. He has a cine camera. The film still exists. Shaky stutterings from way back.

In my back garden, sheets are drying, large white sheets. And there, over there, bordering the small square lawn on each side are the rose bushes. The roses' leaves are serrated.

The girl next door is my age (yippee doodle dandy). Now we are seven years old. She is wearing a black leather pinafore dress. I am in red shorts and a white t-shirt. She is my best friend and she still goes to ballet. Her mother takes her after school. She calls me 'my fat friend'; she is 'my thin friend'. Once we are allowed to camp in a tent in her garden overnight, but it gets too cold and we creep inside, snuggle into the bunk beds and, one Saturday evening in 1967, we are allowed to sit up late in her back room and watch the Eurovision Song Contest. Sandie Shaw is singing *Puppet on a String*:

I wonder if one day that you'll say that, you care if you say you love me madly...

*

You will have guessed by now that in this small room I have a slightly strange responsibility: to speak about things. Though now, as so often, I don't know what to say. How can I say to B those back gardens open to white sheets, snow, roses always? And how, in spring, the wind strews cherry blossom across them both? Pale pink ghosts.

Well, I wonder what you associate with the word 'royal'? B says at my continuing silence.

And now I am too shy to mention *Once in Royal David's City*, my favourite hymn... *stood a lowly cattle shed where a mother lay her baby...* oh, so, so tenderly, and the night-lights, the only light in the darkened church hall on Christmas Eve, and how I walked there with not a mother, but *my* mother, my hand slipped into the fur-warm crook of her arm. Like I did whenever, in winter, we walked to the shops together. And how when it was snowing she wore that beaver lamb fur coat and her flat little brown ankle boots with silver zips up the front and the sheep's wool lining curling out at the top. And how if ever I see boots like those nowadays... Or how worried I am at school when the powder paint tin simply has a white label with black letters 'BLUE' and I can't tell the teacher that my painting will be all wrong as I need r roy... because if the word shaping on my tongue rounds itself out I know I will cry. And I am sure, surer than the sun and the roses and the tyre tracks, surer even than snow itself, that my father's in hospital and I mustn't cry...

Perhaps, B says, *we need to go on thinking about 'royal'... what it means for you?*

I cannot speak. The session ends in my silence. I leave the small room, go down the stairs, open the huge brass latch and pull the door twice to close it behind me. Outside, two more steps and the chinks of the black wrought iron gate opening, shutting. In Brow Road I text my friend:

Today is the happiest day of my life.

*

In B's small room, only the two of us, I am always the one expected to speak first. To begin with, this is straightforward in a way, since there are the facts. Sometimes it is easier to state facts. Facts have a simple way of corresponding to chronology. Events and dates. This happened and that happened and this is when. So here goes:

In 1965 my father tried to kill himself. In 2011 I am admitted to hospital – a psychiatric ward. I am there for twelve days. In 2012 I am, again, admitted to the same hospital, a different ward but still psychiatric. I am there for just over twenty-four hours. August 12th 2012. My father's birthday.

And even before I begin to write anything else I realise how little of this story will actually carry the simplicity of event and date. The events of 1965 and those of 2011 and 2012 are entwined in ways that facts alone fail to reveal.

One of the reasons for this lies simply around how you see truth. I was four years old. My mother has told me what happened. I can't say if it is true. And I can't say it isn't. It's not that I don't believe my mother. Of course I do. But somehow it is more subtle than that. When I think about the things she says, nothing happens in me. I reach a blank. I don't feel anything. I am simply hearing words. Her words. Words that have everything to do with me, but – and I don't know this for a long time – these words have shut me off from myself. I don't have my own words. Only hers. My words are somewhere else. And wherever that is is dammed up. No Entry signs everywhere.

Bereft of my own words, I am convinced, despite B's repeated *facts won't help with what is going on in your internal world...* what I need are facts. In the small room, its neutral greens calming, I will have to learn, facts don't turn out to be the certainties they seem. And I will learn my story, like most stories, is half-truth, half-imagined.

Facts are, however, where I start in the first meeting with B:

My father tried to kill himself... I was four years old. He was taken first to the emergency department at Orpington Hospital. Then to St Francis... and then, finally, to the Maudsley.

And I have had some kind of a breakdown, I was hospitalised in March... for about twelve days, I'm not allowed to drive... I don't have a job anymore...

I had worried about my job, before the pre-term meeting with the Head. Wondering was I overly anxious because my father kept losing his all those years ago? Isn't this just my anxiety taking over? Illness like this, like mine, it's not treated the same way now, is it?

You shouldn't have had to give up your job... B says, *that's sad...*

I am surprised but don't say, surely I couldn't have kept my job? I don't deserve work. How could I? I have been in a psychiatric ward! Are you living in the same world? Her expensive clothes, her lovely house, the proud, black, polished front door with its self-announcing brass knocker tell me, of course, that she is not. She is in a world of liberal ideas, humanist belief and, as I think then, seeped in that middle-class love affair with the sexy, glamourised, commercially marketable, talented mad. The Van Goghs, the Virginia Woolfs, the Sylvia Plaths, each with their unique kaleidoscope of madness and creativity that is so enticing, exciting to read, watch films about. And, yes, whilst I do try and write poetry – a sure sign of madness these days – this isn't quite the same as the settled into canon of the famously mad, is it? I wonder what B knows, really knows about a psychiatric ward. The economically impoverished (mostly) who range between the catatonic silent to the seared and screaming and all the other mads in-between. But I, I have actually been in one only a few months ago and, for all I know, might still even be mad. Isn't it exactly because I am not that talented, not one of the greats that seduce the imagination, that surely I, shame personified, should crawl away into the dark, pain-filled hole of non-existence and never show myself again to the light of people, work, friends, family, enjoying the huge benevolent sun of ordinariness?

Of course I will come to learn slowly, whilst there might be some truth in this, B is not really like this at all. And that she is trained, has more knowledge than I can begin to understand in the raw immediacy of my state and, most of all (and I must repeat this over and over again since there are times when it doesn't feel like this) she is there to help me.

And at first, somewhat absurdly, I believe she is there to help me find out the facts about what happened with my father one Saturday in January 1965. It torments me. I want to know, to know exactly what happened. To know where he was when it happened, to know where I was. I want to know all the details. (I have recorded in my journal: I feel like I am in a detective story. Where was he when it all happened? In the hall? The kitchen? Where was I?) and I wonder now, too, about my younger brother, my older sister. Where were they? Were we, as my mother said, all downstairs playing? I want to know, I want to know, and, as juries say, I want to know beyond all reasonable doubt. Absurd as this is, I think B can tell me.

B is exhausted long before I am. How many times and ways she tries to move me forward out of my need for facts:

What do you associate with the word 'royal'?

At first, in desperation and, always in the belief that words hold secret securities, I look up the word *fact* in the OED. And when I do, I am taken by surprise: *fact* like all the other words is, of course, perfectly organised, but in a way I don't expect. What am I expecting? Well, something like: *event that happened with corresponding date for verification, to be in no doubt about, open to scrutiny and confirmed as the case.* Something like that. What I find is, *fact* as *relating primarily to action*; in the second, *relating to truth.* Here the definition of the word is more precise than I could have imagined. *Truth* and *action*: I am obsessed by both. The truth about an action. But, for the word *relating* – a body thrown overboard – I need a lifebelt.

And, before I'd been into hospital, I thought I was in *the knowing of.* I thought I knew the whole story about my father. I had even told a few people. This story was my possession. Though what is it to own a story, believe it is the truth? Not even as the dictionary says about fact:

relating to truth. No, the story I had *was* the truth. My mother tells me over and over, 'Your dad was taken first to the emergency department at Orpington, then to St Francis... and Dr Scott said she would seek the best possible treatment. She was such a good doctor, eventually she got him admitted to the Maudsley. He was in hospital for twelve solid months...'

But what is it to know also, somehow, far off, dimly glimpsed, you might be dispossessed: that this story, which she had repeated again and again, is split and frayed? What is it to know, so many years afterwards, the threads are unravelling?
It is to lose your mind.
Which I did.

*

To go back to the beginning, as far as really starting to trust B that is, I would have to mention the red scarf. In our first meeting though, I don't trust her. I talk about the doctorate – another fact of my life.

I got it a couple of years before all this happened.

Well, perhaps, it is to do with that? Finishing...? It's a big thing for people, you know, something they have carried for years and then it's gone. A kind of mourning often follows...

Yes, yes, maybe that's it, it has something to do with finishing the doctorate...

The recollection of writing, handing in and being awarded a doctorate is a shadow on the wall of the cave. Since then I have left the cave, stared at the sun and seen the black ring around it.

And, like everyone, I begin lying on the couch, but before too long, a few weeks perhaps, I decide lying on the couch is not something I can continue to do. B is interested:

Why not?

I feel too vulnerable. I know it sounds mad, but I think you are going to hurt me.

Each session, too, there's this bloody Chinese water drop in my mind – thlop, thlop – over and over again, torturing. What to say? I walk up to Brow Road too aware of my heart... What the bloody hell am I to say? B is consistent:

Whatever comes to mind...

But I can't speak.

There are no words for this. Some things you know by osmosis; things that slither around somewhere out of sight and mind, watery. Things that come up like great slippery fish, gulp, and then disappear again, leaving dark tremulous circles. And in that somewhere you know, know that you don't know, but what, for the sake of your sanity, you must try to recall. When I think of my father, it's his gentleness, and his gentleness with me especially, that's uppermost. His manner and his quiet voice. His gentleness, and his hands. He took pride in his beautiful, broad hands. Right at the end of his life, the nurse in the care home said, 'He's a gentleman, your dad, a real gentleman.' But, at the age of thirty-nine, to say it in an old-fashioned way, he tried to take his life by his own hand. Like Sylvia Plath, I cannot put my father together not precisely, *not pieced, glued, and properly jointed,* because I don't remember what happened.

Even I become exhausted, finally, by my quest for facts. Eventually, I come to understand what B means but, as I've said, it takes a long time to learn my story isn't a story about facts. It is a story of knowing and the *not knowing of...* And it takes even longer to learn this is a story about me, myself, I. And that there are many parts to this I:
I-the-puppet, who doesn't know, and I-the-puppet-master who is terrified of the knowing rising up, out of control.
And there is She-who-knows.
And She-who-knows has always known, and her knowledge, multitudinous, lies ocean wide, ocean deep, and, sometimes, her knowledge surges and breaks in waves of strange eloquence.

To begin with, I-the-puppet knows nothing of She. Slowly in the talk with B they will meet in the story of I-who-is-becoming. The talk with B in the small room is somehow indirectly, so very indirectly, the way to heal. Yes, B is there to help I-the-puppet who is in the *not knowing of,* meet the She-who-knows and to help to discover the I-who-is-becoming.
B and the small room are the way to remembering. Memories surface, incidents, words recalled from way back: the necessary flotsam and jetsam. Stories abound. Which words will be retrieved to tell the right story? Even the facts shift prismatically to tantalise. Hold them up one way and it seems for a deceptively pure moment you know, know what happened. And it is clearly the truth. But then you dream. And She-who-knows swims her way up, pushes her head through the water – her eyes staring and her scales silver. Glittering. And it's then you begin to wonder. What if She-who-knows comes out of the water and is glimpsed in the light? Behind the black door, with its brass knocker at B's house where there are many stories, you will find, as I did, the plenitude of stories simply increases your desire to settle on one. The right one.

And for me, and B perhaps, that story starts with the red scarf.

*

I am sitting now in the chair B usually has for herself. She sits, instead, opposite me at one end of the couch. When I give her the red scarf, B spreads it out carefully, thoughtfully. Her fingers are slow and circumspect as she slowly eases out the creases. I am watching her intently. Somehow, this is a kind of test. I think she knows this. And although I know it is a test, I don't know what it means to pass since I don't really know why this scarf matters. Only that it does. I grabbed it and took it with me to the hotel and then the hospital. I knew I had to have it with me. But no words come to say why. No words at all. Whatever else I did, this was a doing in the *not knowing of.* The puppet-master losing control and the sea siren, She-who-knows, strangely singing.

I took it with me to the hospital... I laid it on the heater next to my bed. Over the gaps...

Have you ever worn it?

No, I saw it one day in a charity shop and wondered if it would lighten a black jacket I have, though I decided against it.

It's very red with lots of eyes, B says, her hands smoothing the scarf.

The careful way she does this, the thoughtfulness in her voice, all mean she has passed the test. How badly I need this singular attention, this demonstration of care. In this small room I am freed. Somehow I know for the first time I bought it because I was unable to take my eyes away from the red.

I know, as B spans her fingers over the red, she's taking me seriously. She knows it is of consequence. And I know consequently I, too, am of consequence. I will begin to matter to her.

I glance at the bookcase in B's room. There's a journal lying there. Its red and black cover and its elongated type face is authoritative, proper. Then I stare at the little round table with curved edges – how often my fingers will trace along them as a way of distracting myself and as a way of not looking at B. On it is a box of tissues. I seldom use them. I don't wish to cry in this room, although I am thinking of the hotel room, the narrow bed, the mirror that seemed to both accuse and support me. I know I had a small case with me, my iPad, yes, definitely, and, because the next day I was taken to hospital, I must also have had the red scarf. I must have seized it from the drawer, stuffed it somewhere in my case, or in a pocket perhaps, though I can't remember doing it. I do know, though, I put it over the heater in the hospital. And now B has spread it out and spoken about it, I see, I mean, really see, as if for the first time, not just the eyes, not just the red, but that black edging: zig-zag, jagged.

And, even so, I have no words.

In the coming months, still in shock, I talk about, indeed I obsess about, having no job. B is patient, very patient, but eventually says,

I have never known anyone place so much importance on a job... Isn't there anything today, anything else that you...?

A pause. I don't know her and I don't know if I can trust her, really trust her, to understand my experience. Me. Anything. But I want this to work. I am desperate. I take a risk.

I play chess.

And it is true. Not at first, but by the time I have started to see B about six months after coming out of hospital, it is all I do: I play chess. More in the shock of not having my job than anything else, I cannot read anything at all. For at least a year, not able to read, I no longer know who I am. I can't read, I am not safe. Attempting to read, I am anxious there may be something in a book, any book, that will terrify me. So I join an internet site and play chess with Russians, Chinese, Romanians, and Indians. Sitting by the fire, there's winter in the dimming of the light, my self-flaying thins out, the who-am-I question is silenced. My nervous system, a taut high wire, relaxes. Shame has crawled under the chair, curled up, and is, cat-like, asleep. Life has become my mother's confident fiat about words on a page: black and white. My queen is frontline, proud and demanding. Too aggressive, too early in the game, a Russian tells me. No subtlety. Slowly though, the pieces show their strengths, soldiers in an army, each skilled in its own sphere. I like the chequered, aerial view on screen and find it easier to imagine more moves ahead. I am in another world; the only one I can hold in my mind, understand and act in. One Saturday I play fifteen games one after the other. My nervous system – lightning in storm – is, once again, soothed. When I finally stop, on holiday in Greece, I will have played 1,300 games.

B is about to say something about this remark, but I add suddenly, to my surprise and to hers too...

Once, I was very young, maybe three or four, when she was hanging washing out in the garden, I was sitting on the floor in the kitchen but I got up, went over to the door and I locked my mother out...

Well, that sounds a more interesting you... something rebellious...

Is it rebelliousness too, or something else altogether, that makes me say what comes to mind next?

My mother said Dad used a bread knife.

*

Psychosis. When I ask my doctor for my hospital records I read *psychosis* after the word *diagnosis* on the NHS form. And it's written (as my mother would have pointed out to ensure this ruled out all possible doubt) 'in black and white. Look there!' The dismissiveness in her tone said *make no mistake about it, you surely can't be so stupid as not to understand.* But, as on so many occasions when I was a child and my mother said things, I didn't understand. *Don't be cross with me, Mum, please don't let that irritation bloom in your voice yet again.* Now, once again, I must be stupid, really stupid, because I don't know what this word means.

After I have seen my records I go immediately to the NHS website, and revisit endlessly, reading and reading the same words as if they will, finally, give me something more tangible, something that will settle into an *oh, I see that's what it is*, understanding. The site has been updated recently. It now adds a helpful opening sentence: someone who develops psychosis will have their own unique set of symptoms and experiences, according to their particular circumstances. And four main symptoms are associated with a psychotic episode:

- *hallucinations*
- *delusions*

- *confused and disturbed thoughts*
- *lack of insight and self-awareness.*

Though I can't relate these simple statements to what happened to me.

Perhaps this is because I haven't really understood the nature of truth. Truths. I haven't understood the way from one direction the light shines on ordinary things: a desk, a fruit bowl on the table, a railway track laid out on a carpet, or from another, the east, say, as the sun rises and now it's the garden's roses that are caught, their colour-frilled clarity taking your eye. They are what make you wonder.

One truth is I left hospital with a word written about me and yes, in black and white, but a word that no-one at any point uses to tell me what is wrong with me. The nurse who speaks to me before I am discharged talks of what she calls 'my journey' since arriving in hospital and tells me not to hurry back to work. My own GP thoughtfully, sensitively, wonderfully, asks me what to say on his note to the school where I teach. We settle on 'severe stress, emotional breakdown'. But I have not heard, not even once, the word that will confront me on the formal medical notes when I get them: *psychosis*.

And when I do, for all my years of reading, for all my education, I have no idea what this word actually means.

Why doesn't anyone say? I go to Wikipedia. Psychosis is a noun, the plural: psychoses. The definition: *a severe mental disorder in which thought and emotions are so impaired that contact is lost with external reality*. The categorical certainty of these words frightens me. But the roots of the word, I discover, are more reassuring, coming from the Greek psukhōsis*: animation*, which comes apparently from psukhoō*: I give life to*, from psukhē: *soul, mind*. This makes more sense to me. Something closer to my experience.

In the confusing clasp of this contradiction – an *impairment* and an *animation* – I am desperate to understand what has happened to me, to try to stop my heart knocking at my ribs and to try to stop that huge black JCB tyre of shame which is rolling over me, crushing me, leaving its tread imprinted on my whole body, my whole existence.

But the only thing I read, in the days after I leaving hospital the first time, that keeps me in any way hopeful, is this simple statement: *the mystic and the psychotic inhabit the same space*. It is the only thing that seems to hold me from drowning in a sea of all the other words. A suggestion of greater insight. A knowing, that is present in all the *not knowing of*. I cling to this one insight – a raft, after shipwreck.

And now, you have to understand how suddenly madness came upon me the first time. How it seemed to begin with the sky. Looking up at the night sky. Yes, the sky, this is a beginning... (Although there are other beginnings, always different places to begin, I learn that in the sessions, time and events in the kaleidoscopic shift between sanity and madness, turn, settle to stranger, less familiar patterns and, even then, turn again.) That evening, a Thursday perhaps, like many other ones, I take a walk around the block. The two roads I often walk along just before going to bed. I observe the moon's brightness, the sky's occult dark, the stars, and, through it all, a powerful swirling wind, which somehow also feels private as if for my eyes only. If someone had told me there was no wind, would I have believed what was said? Perhaps they could not see this – the wind that opened the secrets of the world. This wind rushed through the trees and seemed to be the living spirit of the world. Not just the elements in their elemental power, but something more, stronger, clearer, revelatory – the living energy of everything. The physics books say the world and everything in it is all energy, and so it appeared to me. Energy. Shimmering lights: lights as vital, pulsating energy. And wind streaming through everything – *Spiritus Mundi. The breath of the world.*

The next day, I am in the bathroom, bent over the basin and my body is no longer in my control. My hips seem to be pulled out from behind me and a shaking begins from the bottom of my spine and goes all the way through me up to my head, which is shaken from side to side so vigorously my cheeks and jaws are also shaken and my mouth, flaccid, makes a brrr, brrr, as if shivering after coming out of very cold water. I hear this brrr, brrr, as if it is far away and soon my whole body is bent over the basin shaking. Then, as if some power has seized my arm, I begin to write in the notebook I have brought into the bathroom. I am demented with creative ideas for a poem. I write furiously fast, scrawling illegibly, punning, some letters huge, others small, and then suddenly, surprisingly, in perfectly controlled letters, perfectly legibly – a new word on each page: *spirit guides, shamans, oracles, prophets, diviners of the divine, star gazers,* and then in the smallest writing of all, on its own page, halfway down: *the snow has no voice.* Then I draw one thin line straight down the middle of another page. After that, the writing breaks down and becomes minute strokes of carefully drawn shapes, my arm no longer under any control of mine, but drawing all the same and not in any way I could ever repeat. Some of these images, even today, even with all the work in the small room, I still don't understand.

The day after, a Saturday, I am in the bathroom again. I am clapping and singing: *Swing low, sweet chariot coming for to carry me home...* And I begin arranging everything in the bathroom in threes, as if two adults were on either side of a baby, and I believe it is Moses in a basket in the middle. Actually there were only soaps, shampoo bottles, flannels, deodorant, cleansers, the blue and white tube of Savlon. (*That's very Oedipal*, says B much later when I describe this to her… *everything laid out in threes.*) The picture we have by the painter, Munch, on the bathroom wall of a woman dressed in white with long red hair looking out over water, I believe to be my mother in spiritual preparation for death. I know, in my frenzied state, she is preparing for death and that, if I can, I must open the window to let her soul depart. Then I put a towel and our Paul Klee print of the pink house into a laundry basket. I know I need it to cleanse my parents' house. Purify it.

In the afternoon we are going out for tea at the Grand Hotel, 3.00 pm. I warn Francis, my partner, 'You will have to call the ambulance. There will be a lot of blood.' Sitting in the car with one hand on the steering wheel I urge my mother to cut her throat, 'Go on, yes, you can do it.' Then time itself splits and disappears. I stare at the sun without blinking. See the black ring around it. And scream.

By Sunday morning I have locked myself in a toilet at the local sport's club. I am moving my fingers across the tiles by the door slowly towards the light above the cistern. All the time I know, know that I must run my fingers along the cracks and no matter what, however long it will take, despite the cleaner knocking on the door, and my 'just a minute, I won't be long,' no matter – I must get to the light. The light. I am in the toilet for a long time. The cleaner calls again, and again I say cheerfully, 'won't be long.'

'I sat with you for several hours,' the club manager says to me afterwards when she allows me re-admission to the club once I have left hospital. I don't remember her being with me at all. I do remember someone touching me saying, 'it's alright dear' as she came out of the showers. I remember saying, very angrily, to a woman who was putting on make-up, 'you don't need that.' And to a small girl, 'you are beautiful just as you are; don't you ever let anyone tell you otherwise.' And I remember the police car and the ambulance when I am walked out of the club entrance. At the hospital (I am told afterwards) I am shouting. I see a woman wheeled in wearing an oxygen mask. Is she my mother? I believe she is. I see an old man in the green-curtained cubicle. Is he my father? I believe he is. I know that they have a spiritual illness. I know that all the people in this ward have spiritual illnesses, not physical ones. We are, I believe, on the lowest floor of the hospital and everyone there is being given panaceas because, actually, they are not physically unwell, they are spiritually ill. In my strange state, I know their spirits are impeded.

I am sedated, given a brain scan. The doctor tells Francis, 'you might as well go, she'll sleep now until the morning.' The next day I am allowed home. I have, apparently, 'gone off like a shaken-up coke bottle'. He says I should see my own doctor.

(B shakes her head in dismay when, later in the small room, I tell her all this, and simply says: *So irresponsible...*)

A day or so after the doctor has sent me home, I drive myself to a hotel and check in. And already as I think about it now I ask who was that 'I'? The perpendicular pronoun a colleague used to call it, but who exactly does it refer to? I-the-puppet or I-the-puppet-master? Neither. They can't recognise it is She, She-who-knows, knows the deep sea-bed. Yes, it is She. And She is stirring. Somewhere She is singing. Her voice, one of air and water. It is She who drives to the hotel, checks in. The hotel is right by the beach with the breezes that delight the ear and hurt not. I go to my room, a small single room. The smallness of this room makes me think it is a nun's room, a room for the spirit. And She-who-knows, knows this is exactly right.

Now I am a face in the hotel room's mirror. I am a face. Am I the moon's face with its *O gape of complete despair?* Dragging its dark crime like a sea? This face has brown hair. Short. No, not the moon's. It is not a face in its own right. It is the face of the puppet-master and it is determined and it is the face of the puppet and it is nice, attractive. It is wearing foundation and it has lipstick and strings. The puppet-master's strings can lift the mouth ends and turn them up and it can show its white teeth, and it can smile! Yes, it can smile. It really can! And then it is the shorn head of a puppet, the neck jerked round. Yes, it is this odd angled face with bolts in the temples (I find her image later on the computer and take it in to show B) and whose strings might break and who has a thin-felt-sharpness drawn across her throat because she is not supported, and she can't say. There are no words. She has no voice. And her throat hurts since there's this thin-felt-sharpness across it. And her throat glitters and her face is the face of the puppet whose voice, snow-silent, should be screaming.

The next day I leave the hotel, drive to my parents' house. I want to heal the years of their mutually inflicted misery. I want to heal the house, their hearts. I try to get them both to sit on the sofa together. A sort of symbol. But they won't. Someone says something about a doctor. I don't know who. But I say I'll ring for one. I ring 999 and tell my parents.

'What did you do that for, dear?' my father, his tone lame-annoyed.

The ambulance comes, as I think, for my parents. It is me who is taken to hospital instead. My mother follows in her car. We sit in a small pale room. Plastic covered chairs, thin metal arms and a small table in front of me. The woman dealing with me is agitated. I tell her who I am. She looks surprised. 'Perhaps you would like a sandwich? I'll get you one.' And when she comes back, she smiles, somewhat relieved. 'Oh, you are who you say you are, and you have written poems. I checked it out on the internet.' She has brought tea too, in a plastic cup with a small brown plastic frame around it so you can hold it without burning your fingers. One more aid for the disabled. And she talks to me and calls another doctor. I don't know what we talk about. But I do say something about the world, a symbol needed for the world. They decide I need to spend some time in another hospital. 'We've no beds here. I'll contact E– see if they have beds there.' She is back, moments later, pleased. 'Yes. They have. There's an ambulance going over to E–it can take you. Will you be happy to go?' 'Yes,' and I believe in saying it I am admitting myself voluntarily.

The ambulance journey is rather enjoyable. I remember trying to make the ambulance man smile, laugh, enjoy himself. I think there may have been other people in the ambulance too. I think the ambulance man's shoes were black and shiny. He moves them in rhythm, the rhythm of the traffic, the traffic lights jolting him out of it because we kept stopping. We laugh and I sense that he is enjoying this. I am drawing him out of a deep down soul-sea sadness.

When I get to the hospital the doctor asks me:

'Did you think of killing yourself?'

*

I am locked in. I try to persuade a nurse to let me go back to the hotel. 'I will come back in the morning, I promise.' But she will not allow this. I know I am not quite myself; and I know I shouldn't be locked in. I know that they shouldn't be allowed to keep me in hospital. No, I am not quite myself and I am shocked. What am I doing here?

I go down to the small garden, stand there with my arms stretched out and up, an imploring Christ figure, and determine I will stay there all night if necessary. They will see me and then know that I should be allowed out, given my determination to stand there all night. I imagine one of the nurses saying to someone else, perhaps Francis who will have, by then, come to visit, 'She stayed there all night, you know.' The nurse's tone will be one of incredulity and awe. In my fantasy I am admired for my willingness to stand. I stare at the darkening sky and the huge incinerating tower with its small red lights on the top and I stretch my arms out as far as I can. I am very distressed at the thought of all the bandaged bloods, the red and white, burning there, and I am a martyr to my cause.

'Surely someone will let me out of this hospital?' Somewhere inside and far off, I know nothing's going to happen. I tell myself, 'Go inside, you fool, you may as well,' and when I do I meet a nurse.
'Look, I don't want to stay here. I want to go back to the hotel. I promise I will come back in the morning.' The nurse shakes her head, guides me inside to a ward.

A green curtain separates my bed from my neighbour's. I keep it pulled. My bed is next to the window and by it there is a heater. I put my red scarf over it. And this *a not-knowing in the doing of,* since the metal heater has darkness in the downness of its open slits. Open slits cannot be borne. The red scarf lies over them so I am in *the not seeing of.*
When I notice the woman in the bed on the other side of the curtain, I am more distressed. She is comatose. Unwashed, half-undressed. She lies for several days, not moving, not speaking to anyone. I learn she is going to have ECT. This frightens me too. In my mind I have images from films, lines from Plath, and a question mark about it for my father.
'ECT works, you know,' a nurse says. She doesn't ask what I think.

But it destroys your memory, B says when I tell her this. And, by then, I know the very sharp significance of this remark.

Opposite me in the ward there's a young woman. She has more than enough weight, demure, pale-skinned – a large injured cat in its lair. Hair, coppery blonde. Doesn't say anything; cries, cries, cries. Then she speaks to me as if I can bring it about: 'I want to see my children. I want to see my children.' She says it in a mean-no-harm-to-anyone, the injustice-of-it, an-out-of-the-window-jump voice.

When she repeats herself for the third time, like some crowing cock, I remember with, not denial, but honesty, what I had said to the doctor on arrival: 'Yes, for about three minutes... in the hotel... I did think about it...'

Another young woman roams the corridors day and night in her dressing gown crying. Not speaking or looking. Crying and crying. Hair, long, matted, wire-bundled. Her face a perpetual red squall.

And then there is Sharon. Sharon is vocal and forthright. She has long brown hair, a pudgy face, small eyes, the intelligent eyes of a pig. Staring, blue – both seeing and unseeing. Thirty five?

‘Are you Princess Diana? Are you Princess Diana?’ she calls persistently to me down the corridor. When Francis comes to visit me she cries out at him, ‘Are you the Pope? Are you the Pope? I have fucked the Pope.’

By that time, the noise in the ward stopping me from sleeping, I have been given my own room. I am checked on at night. A slit opens in the door. I usually wake. Someone looks in. I hadn’t quite understood at first when Francis said: ‘They want to give you your own room, you just need more rest. Some more sleep and you’ll be fine again.’ I am delighted to have my own room. I have my books and a journal so I am content. Besides there is little else to do. We are all unwell in here, but why don’t they give us things to do? The fitness room is closed. I think it had a few weights inside and doubled as a meditation room, but never opened while I was there. I stare out of the window at the lumpy grass, the odd flower, and long to see the area properly cultivated. Cared for. How different it would be here if this was a garden. As a bird flies over, I know for sure the planet is dying, as I have just seen blood on the bird’s wing. Later I tell B and know she is right when she says, *a projection.*

Sharon has her own room too. Her mother visits. Sharon’s room is quiet, then, ‘...don’t wan... don’t wan... don’t wan... wailing’. And, from my room at the end of the corridor, I can hear the wailing in Sharon’s room.

Although it is a couple of hours later when there is a knock at the door.

Sharon, still wailing,
'My hair... my h, h, hair... she's...my h, h, hair...'
'What Sharon? Sharon, who?'
'Thinks I am a baby...'
'What's happened? Sharon, what is it? I don't quite understand.'
'She's cut my hair. She's cut my hair. I di'n wan' it cut... not, not, not a baby.'
Sharon tugs at short curls. Her mother's cut her hair. In the *not knowing of*, but with pain far-down like hers, I hug her and I pray to a God I don't ordinarily believe in. 'Please God heal her. Please, please God stop her pain.' Sharon becomes calmer and stops wailing. She takes off the silver necklace she is wearing and gives it to me. 'You are Princess Diana!'

*

B's practice. Brow Road. Where I am walking to. The first time, many times. Out of the station, right, cross at the lights. One foot, heavy-heaved, flat-fall, the other heavy-heaved, flat-fall. Breath, hill-catching. No pavement, just a low metal barrier – metallic eye-dead silver buckled by smash. My puppet-master self making my puppet-self walk. And although Brow Road is pleasant enough, sunlight, trees, cars, a skip, parking meters, the odd gull or dove, in my head there's the image of the moon from Plath's poem and *I simply cannot see where there is to get to...*

Plath's words speak to and for me. I took *Ariel* with me to hospital. The notes I sent to the expressionless Indian consultant, who simply closed his eyes when I was talking to him, were Plath's too. *So Herr Docktor...*

It seems, I learn later from my hospital records, I wrote quite a lot of notes, I shouted and I talked a lot, to others, to myself, and I lacked insight. I lacked insight, it would seem, into my own behaviour. Certainly I-the-puppet-master lacked insight into what all this was about. Underneath this strange behaviour, I will come to learn, was terror.

And, is it because terror might swim upstream from cold water that I don't know what to say in the small room and, instead, I-the-puppet-master am obsessed with facts and word definitions?

I looked up 'royal' when I got home... I tell B. She rolls her eyes.

Only sometimes do sessions carry over from one day to the next. Today I ensure it does. I unfold my piece of paper and read it to her. This, incidentally, is a development. I have, until now, just handed any piece of paper to B without saying anything. And watched closely as she glances first at the bottom of the page and goes to the top, then skim reads very quickly. She doesn't really like things being written down in the way I have been doing: to explain things. She wants me to talk. Find the words. She is trying to read the subtext, the links I make. The way I am making associations. But today there's only the definition which I read aloud:

Royal: befitting or appropriate to a monarch, esp. in quality, size, or ostentation; stately, magnificent, splendid, imposing.

Anything else?

I miss her irony.

Well, I suppose... and I smile *...it's not surprising but... 'royal', not really my blue coat, but the word itself... well, in here at least, it makes me think of Oedipus...*

Don't ask me why, but the first time I read the story of Oedipus I imagined a dovecote. I had been to Greece, seen one there. A square stone dovecote, a little way down a narrow track just off the road as it turns, just before the three roads meet and Oedipus calls out to the passing carriage 'Get out of my way.' Just before he unwittingly kills Laius, his father. Now I wonder where, in the mind, does Oedipus put his murder of the ageing man, his father – the old man he believes to be a traveller of no consequence? As much as the story rests on forgetting, the unfolding story of Oedipus also rests on memory, a necessary remembering: the spilling of his father's blood.

The dovecote helps me place the story in time. Not long ago and far away, but a time which really is my time, and there's a small faded brown wooden door, and a pile of rough-hewn stones on one side. On the other, where the grass is straw-yellow, dried from the sun, a tall cypress tree. It's green. A dark foreboding. The drystone wall curves round it separating it from the road. The sky arcs blue. On top of the dovecote when I pass are some of the doves, others are on the ground. They look ordinary. Their tail feathers flick in the slight breeze. They peck in quick, nervous movements, with none of the grace they have in the sky. Ordinary white birds. As ordinary as the chickens that later will strut proprietarily across the road in front of the car, or the cockerel that will call the dawn in each morning. But, as Oedipus is approaching, it is the light that takes my attention, the sheer, lucid cut of the light. And, as I say *Oedipus* in the session, I-who-is-becoming, realise B's words, those very particular words about the red scarf, very red with lots of eyes, opened some dark, silent ravine in my mind into that light. The imagination's sharp light. The kind of light in which trees, rocks, dovecotes, doves can be mistaken – not ordinary light. Cleaved.

My father – suddenly I remember this too – tells me one day about how he cared for a dove he'd found. The war's on, the dove pipping milk from a pipette. 'Took a long time for the dove to trust me.' My father never spoke about the war except for two things: to say to my younger brother when he was being silly, 'At your age, boy, I was in charge of men twice my age!' And, 'You don't know what it's like to come home and open the front door, see the back of the house has been blown off.'

Loss of his home was a fear that never left him, though perhaps it eased when my brother helped pay off his mortgage. 'He was homeless, when I met him, you know...' my mother tells me in another of her stories, '... sleeping in the YMCA. After his mother died he was sent to boarding school and didn't go home in the holidays – he was only nine years old then and his father had him stay all alone in B & B's... terrible for a child to be so alone... so he never had a home after that, until we got married... And that night in Soho, after they told him he'd lost his job, well he just kept saying 'Promise you'll never leave me..., promise you'll never leave me. I don't think now, it was because he loved me... really he was terrified of having no home.'

My father's eyes are a soft, proud grey. His voice soft too, telling of the dove cosseted, trusting him. I am happy when he tells me this – the dove, something he'd loved. I imagine his broad hands, the pulsing nervousness at the dove's throat, my father's tenderness. He stutters on the word as he speaks, 'Gath, gath, gathering its strength, it finally flew away...'

Is that why there were doves in my madness?

*

Perhaps it's fear of being alone with your own thoughts... you have to keep an eye on me, perhaps that's why you don't want to lie on the couch... if you do, well, it's less like a conversation, freer, more scope to follow your own mind as thoughts arise... but perhaps you aren't easy with... what did Keats call it... something being in uncertainties, mysteries, doubts, without, B moves her hand to find the words... *reaching after fact and reason...*

Negative capability...

And it is one of the things that mark our early sessions, how much they are conversations full of cultural references. And she is right to mention uncertainties, mysteries, doubts since I-the-puppet-master am, once again, quickly back to my bootless quest for facts.

I am thinking of getting my father's records... From the doctor... I will ask my dad's permission, of course... I think it will help.

B is understanding, but sceptical.

It won't settle what's going on in your internal world...

But don't you see, I only remember a couple of things...

I pause to see if she is interested, listening, attending. Attention is a form of love. And I need that kind of love. B waits quietly until I start to speak again.

I only remember the glare and flash of blue light – the ambulance's...

Though I don't actually say each time since *explosions, implosions* – head and heart at the sound or sight of any ambulance.

... the fluorescent strip light... the fluorescent light was flickering... we had a long thin fluorescent light in the kitchen... and there was this elephant's foot umbrella stand... After my dad did what he did (what B and I go on to refer to in our sessions, as 'the event'). *Mum says she went in the ambulance with my dad to the hospital and we were taken across the road to some neighbours – the Joltons. Mrs Jolton was a nurse and he was a colonel... they'd been to India, both of them... old colonials, really...*

in their hall... after you went through this very shady green porch, once you got into the house, there was this huge elephant's foot. Wrinkly, grey skin with yellow-tar coloured nails like the fingers of someone who smokes... (I smile at B) *my Dad smoked... the foot had been hollowed out... full of umbrellas. I suppose now, thinking about it, they must have brought it back from India... And, as you know, just before I went into hospital, almost every day I had this thought: I think I saw a lot of blood...*

But that is not quite how it was. How it was, is like this:

A thought which keeps coming – no high-wire high enough to stop it jumping over, no pearls bright enough to throw it into darkness, no water deep enough to drown it. A thought, before I am taken to hospital, which interrupts my thinking about the lamb for supper, the child at work I must speak to, the telephone bill I must pay, the conversation about exams I must have with Mrs D. about Simon's handwriting, his spelling, the book I must read about gifted children and, not only the musts, but the open blue in the sky on a bright day, laughing with a colleague, the violet blue of the mist that fuzzes in from nowhere over the Downs and, driving home, the cars, the traffic lights, the rain, the rapid swirling water on the down side of the bridge, the slipping sun, the new long light strip of horizon on the flood-darkened fields – through it all this thought that wants to be spoken, spoken aloud, wants to be sure, sure of what is uncertain... the uncertainty as disturbing as the thought. True? Why have I never thought this before? Why now this thought? Where has it come from? And, is it attached to fact?

Why now at fifty-one does this thought, break through, up out of the water, silver-hued and glittering? Why does it rehearse itself over and over again, with its knowing eye staring, its tail wild and slashing, the dark circles widening, not disappearing, but quickening, strengthening, becoming more fervent. Why do I want to say it aloud, as if someone, anyone, was listening: *my father tried to kill himself and I think I saw a lot of blood...*

*

Blood, I realise now, was mentioned even in my very first meeting with B. Had I also told her about the blood – that one recurring thought, even then, at that first meeting? I don't know, maybe that was later. And it doesn't matter. I have heard since a psychoanalyst remark that it's all there, everything you need to know is all there in the first session if only you can read it. And indeed it was, and maybe B knew this. All I know is in that first meeting with B blood surfaced in our conversation in the most matter of fact kind of way.

B was outlining her terms, the conditions of the work.

I work on a sliding scale, depending on someone's capacity to pay. And, while we're on the subject, I charge for any missed sessions and that includes illness.

I won't miss any sessions.

And I resolve there and then that if she accepts me, no matter what, I won't miss any sessions. I already had some vague idea about resistance and how someone unable to accept an idea will try to sabotage the work by not turning up. This is a promise to myself which, incidentally, as the work takes its tough shape, I am unable to keep.

The only time I'd miss a session might be if I have a period.

That's alright. You can still come in – it's an all-girl household here.

And immediately I feel daunted she doesn't understand, can't understand, won't ever understand me... I want to say to her, 'Can't you ask me something more...? I want to tell you in the first two days, two nights, yes, two days and two nights, I go through forty super plus tampons and fifteen of the thickest night towels there are!' Instead I simply nod.

Not long after this however, B surprises me. Perhaps this *is* when I say to her: my father tried to kill himself and

I think I saw a lot of blood. Or, perhaps it's when I tell her that my mother thought, since no-one had explained anything to her, she was dying with tuberculosis when she had her first period. Or perhaps B's intriguing remark is made when I show her the red scarf. After all, it doesn't take much for either of us to see the very red scarf as blood, even if we don't say so.

Later on in our sessions, when I am a little more relaxed, I try to explain about my periods. How heavy they are, how sometimes I can barely stand up, how I bleed through the heaviest tampons and a night towel in twenty minutes wearing both together. How I am white-faced. 'Are you alright, girl?' Even at seventeen, my French teacher at school has stopped me in the corridor, 'You look like that wall over there...' She is pointing at the newly-painted white outside the staffroom. How I can't think a thought in my exams because my brain is bled dry. How Francis calls me 'Seneca's wife.' I smile at B:

Seneca's wife tried to kill herself in a bath, and although she survived ever after she always looked so white from loss of so much blood.

And I tell B about how, years later, I am diagnosed with anaemia yet again. How the private doctor dismisses me when I suggest I might be anaemic. 'You're not anaemic! Why, your hair would have fallen out and your nails would be turning up.' But I insist on a check and, after the results come through, he phones on a Saturday evening, 'You are anaemic, very anaemic! I can't believe you have been going into work with iron levels that low...'

From then on I take heavy duty iron tablets every day.

But I can't say that I sleep on a dark red towel, so the blood won't show... And I can't describe the terror of the dark, red-filled toilet bowl... Oh, and I can't say, I get up three times a night, four, more... blood on my nightdress, sheets, duvet, mattress, slippers... that I can't move... and that I am weeping... and I can't say... can't say... can't say blood smells? And do you, do you know what the smell is? Even so, B's next comment surprises me.

Anything to do with blood, especially blood outside the body can be frightening, really frightening... for all of us... blood is supposed to be inside, but the body finds its place of weakness to express its pain. I expect your heavy periods and the event with your dad are linked...

How can this be? That thought immediately contradicted by another. Yes, she is right. Somehow glimpsed far away in the sun dipping into the sea, there is a stirring of possibility, a strangeness reverberating that makes a kind of sense, that the river of weakness in me runs through my body down into a blood-dark ocean.

I nod. B is right, but I don't know in what way. Because I can't say – because there aren't joined up letters, there isn't joined up speech, my father *isn't glued and properly jointed...* And I can't say: the smell of blood is metallic.

But I don't know... did I see a lot of blood? I don't know if that's true... I have to know the facts. The facts. What actually happened. Don't you see how very important it is?

And I am still affording B so much knowledge, so much wisdom, so much expertise I think she will be able to tell me. That she will, because of her experience, her training, her knowledge of the world, her ability to read the mind, be able to tell me.

I don't know what really happened... I can't read minds, she says, as if she has actually just done exactly that.

But don't you understand, why don't you understand? Wouldn't you want to know, if it were you? Imagine your son – I know B has a son and I know that isn't quite the same, but it's the nearest analogy I can come up with – *disappeared and everyone said he was dead, wouldn't you want to know actually whether he really was or not...?*

B is too sensible to be provoked. We sit together quietly with our own thoughts.

My fingers find the curved edges of the little table. I look straight ahead without speaking. Outside the light slips – for certainty, for the fact that I wasn't forgotten, lost, in *the darkness of,* in his *distance away of*: the car park, the street, the shop, the beach, my father, arm outstretched, his broad, beautiful hand, waving...

*

It is raining. The rain makes a fast fuzz on the tyres of the cars as I drive to B's. B opens the door. Stands there for a moment to greet me. Welcoming certainly, but assured too. Gathered. I go upstairs before her. I like being welcomed into the house, into her house. I imagine it is how my mother would greet me, in the family life we didn't have. My mother would open the door, smile at me, ask me about my day at school, give me my favourite snack. Merrily, merrily. B opening the door lets me into her house and into the mother at home, the mother welcoming her child back from school, that phantasy. Somehow the two merge and, perhaps, this is the point. I go upstairs quite quickly. There is the chair on the landing and bookcases; the titles catch my eyes, intrigue me. But I can never remember them. Something on Proust this time? There is a photo of a green plant, the greens I couldn't stop staring at just before the second time I went to hospital. The carpet is a kind of coir. I like it. There is a plant and a lamp on the stairs and, at the top, there is the loo. I always go to the loo before the session starts. It is immaculate, clean and cool. A simple hand towel, beige or grey, over the rail underneath a glass shelf. On the glass shelf there is a glass tumbler with a blue crystal circle around the top. It makes me think of my childhood marbles. The more ordinary marbles had flecked eyes of greeny-grey or yellow or red inside them, some were pure crystal or bottle green and larger or smaller, and some were opaque, but with a swirl of another colour, maybe a blue with a white spun through. So desirable. Yes, primary school marbles were mesmerising. Something royal about them. Didn't they have different statuses: a princess, a queen, a king? And somewhere I sense roughly cut grass, tufts of it, warm sun and, ever so faintly, the smell of a sweet shop with candy twists, mint bulls' eyes, a small hand reaching, and further away the beach huts on the green and the sea's white-spumed mutterings...

I wash my hands and sip water from this glass sometimes and put it back on the shelf as exactly as I can. Then I glance at the small clock as I enter the room. B is either at the window (perhaps this is to mark the start of the three sessions that week), or she is already sitting on the couch. I sometimes glance quickly over at her. But, most often, I am too shy. She looks over at me. Her eyes are very clear, penetrating. I like them, but I retreat from the power of their gaze. She has beautiful eyes. Green, I think. And sometimes they look at me without blinking. She is not staring, though she is looking at me. Straight in the eyes. I sense presence. That rounded out presence of an older woman. I turn my head down, sometimes almost in the opposite direction to the bookcase next to the chair. I look down at the lowest shelf. Lying flat this time is *On Not Being Able to Paint.* A book I have since dipped into myself. Sometimes I cannot make eye contact at all. I cannot speak. And even though I can't, I feel an immense sense of support. This beautiful woman's sharp, but thoughtful presence. I am held there. After this first look, she slightly lowers her head. A gesture which I understand to be: I am ready. I am listening.

You see, the way it works in the room is to permit the free flight of the mind, my mind, loose it from its correspondence to command. Psychoanalysis might be described as the task of finding a mind of one's own. And the analyst listens and, to help with this, you are not supposed to know anything about the analyst. But, even so, let me tell you more about B. She has black hair. She wears glasses some of the time. She has beautiful clothes: a leather skirt, a mustard jumper, plum suede shoes and, as I have said, beautiful eyes. Before I began coming regularly to her house, letting the brass hand knocker on the smartly painted black door thump twice, then waiting two steps down for her shadow behind the door's glass, I had met her once or twice at a friend's dinner parties. I can't be sure whether it helps or not. I can't look back because then I would feel as if I know what, in our sessions, I should say. And I don't. Or I can't.

So sometimes it's easier for me to begin with a question.

Do you think...? I was wondering if...? Could it be that...?

B has strategies for this.

Well, what do you think? How do you think about that?

I nearly always cringe inside when she turns the question back. I don't know. I want her to tell me.

If you say something, then maybe I can get closer to what I think...

I believe this. She doesn't. Or, sometimes, she says she feels carolled. Her own mind taken over, hemmed in by my question, a way of controlling her thoughts. Making her think about what I want her to think about. Not let her think as she wants to. Sometimes I think there is something in this. Sometimes I don't. And now I have to ask her something for my own understanding:

You said last session that psychosis was the unconscious bursting out, didn't you?

Mm, that's certainly one of the things going on...

She returns to the fact that I have started with a question again. A way, we both begin to see, thanks to her insight, I have to try and discover what she is thinking, another security for me, another way to avoid the contents of my mind. But B knows the work is about the freeing of my mind. The nature of my own mind. Analysis, well, B's kind anyway, Freudian, Kleinian, relies on an enforced not knowing. At first, not knowing anything personal about her at all, I find this lack of reciprocity very difficult. I still ask without meaning to:

Do you?

Are you?

Will you?

If?

A blank. B has all but perfected the blank.

And it seems to me that blank echoes the one in me. The one that I can't find words for. The day in 1965 I can't remember. That huge white blank. White as snow and voiceless. And my madness: an implosion. An explosion. No, the blank inside me is more physical than that. Whatever happened is written in the mind, but it is also written in the body. Psychosis, I am learning, is about memory. It is the implode of mind and body. The explode of body and mind. Headplode. Heartplode. Both the agony of remembering and, at the same time, of the not remembering.

So I try and try again, session after session, to just begin talking, talking about myself. How anxious this makes me. And just talking about myself, I realise I don't know who I am at all. But I try a statement this time, not a question.

I feel like I am a puppet...

B is sitting on the couch and moving her lower leg up and down in a way that she does sometimes. It makes me think she might be nervous.

That's what I am... a puppet. I am good at being a puppet. And I am a good puppet, a very good one.

I smile, self-conscious, at all the 'goods' in these remarks.

My mother always says it about me 'but you were always such a good girl, you know, such a good girl...'

Pause.

Do you remember how I told you that I wrote in very, very small letters in my notebook just before going into hospital 'the snow has no voice'?

And I begin then to tell B about what had happened at the Clarins counter at Boots and how much it pleases me that she is so quick to know, even before I say it, the Clarins uniform is red.

The day's mild, the breeze's warmth consoling. I have been out of hospital for about two months and have to see the doctor for a new prescription. He is warm and kind. I am very lucky. He has known me a long time. I used to teach his children. He reassures me and makes me smile, 'when I first heard you were in hospital I was vaguely surprised.'
We talk about my medication. I tell him I am going to Greece for the early part of the summer. 'Well, that should keep you going...' He prescribes enough tablets to last while I am out there. I am looking forward to it. When I leave he hugs me. I am not cast out. I am not a leper, an untouchable. He'd hugged me! And I like the choice of 'vaguely' in his surprise. I decide later that he mustn't have thought me nuts before all this. This consoles me too.

I walk down from the doctor's to Boots, the Clarins counter, since I need a new mascara to take to Greece.
'Can I help you?'
'Yes, I need a mascara.' I say, strangely irritable now at even being by the Clarins counter.
'Oh, well you've come to the right place. What exactly are you looking for: volumising, high density, lengthening,

waterproof, black, brown, brown-black?' The assistant's name badge says Cathy. She has dark hair.
'Brown, thickening...'
'Well, this one is very popular, one of our best sellers...' Cathy holds up a brush that she has pulled out from a gold cylinder and angles it in front of my face. I am even more irritable.
'Or, perhaps this is better...' Another sludgy pull and this time a thicker exuberance of bristle is held up before me. Is it the level of detail that is irritating me? Symbols of the profligate consumer paradise we inhabit?
'Oh, but we only have that in black, I think. Let me check.' She bends down and rummages in a cupboard under the counter. While she is down there, probably not even a minute, no adjective can give enough weight to 'irritation,' nor is 'irritation' the right word to describe how I am feeling.
'You know, you might find this one exactly what you need.'
A longer, thinner brush, a tapering end.
'Very good for getting in the corners...'
Am I irritated because this assistant, Cathy, has become commercialism personified? How can anyone spend so much effort trying to sell mascara? Such triviality! And for a moment I think it is this triviality that is making me very, very irritable. Inexplicably, I think I am going to scream.

But I know if I scream, scream in the way I want to in the middle of Boots on this May afternoon, the immaculate red-uniformed Cathy will call an ambulance and the store manager will come and grab hold of me until the ambulance arrives to take me back to hospital.

Swallowing, I just grab the first mascara my hand hits upon standing upright in one of the displays instead. 'I'll take this one!' A completely random choice, none of the ones I have been shown so far. For a moment, dark-haired Cathy looks at me askance. Something's going on here, she doesn't quite understand.
'I only have that in brownish-black...'
Her look is enough for me to know that I must calm down. I must summon the polite voice of a satisfied customer. A puppet's voice. Somehow in this department store I have become suddenly aware that I am not entirely, wholly real. I know I/she/girl/woman is conceived as image, as a wooden puppet at the design stage. A puppet who lies on a piece of paper with a sketch of a woman on it. And there are joints and pins on this bald, colourless, wooden puppet. Ready and waiting. And it will soon have strings attached to go out, go shopping. Now in this Boots store, right now, in the middle of E —— I know, really know, that I am a puppet, a puppet hollowed out and emptied of desire. Am I Pinocchio? My nose so long, with the lies of my existence, that it would touch the sky. Why does no-one stare at this nose

of mine? The lies it represents. My steps are halting, unsure. My wooden eyes, so large and blue, see so much. And here, in this department store at the Clarins counter knowing I am puppet, I discover just how much of a puppet I am. I know my limbs are jointed and they suggest movement, but not autonomy, only passivity. And I know those who are not puppets move freely with the surety of heart and body wedded to desire: desire, and the surety of mother love, which is the surety of self. My limbs move only on stringed expectations: of goodness, of care for others, of self-denial, self-punishment, self-abnegation, self-sacrifice, self-flagellation, self-destruction. I am a stuffed puppet, pumped and padded up by pretence. My mouth is stitched in the long black strictures of a smile.

Sometimes the puppet-master – a ventriloquist – gives me words, nice ones, soothing, gentle. The voice is gentle too, soft. And me-the-puppet-master can move my puppet-limbs, my-puppet-master-self nods my puppet head in agreeable agreement. But the puppet doesn't know how to say: 'I want...' 'I need...' doesn't know how to find words, the real words. All I ever hear is my puppet voice as my-puppet-self walks, falteringly, in circles around a made-up stage, dumb circles yanked by my own puppet-master's strings. And sometimes, I-the-puppet have no voice. Worse, sometimes I don't even know I am a puppet. I am simply snow. Blank white snow. And *the snow has no voice.*

My strings are those of being a girl, a girl, a good girl: I have no voice. I-the-puppet am at the Clarins counter in Boots to buy a mascara. Cathy behind the counter is trying to be helpful. She is very well-made up: foundation, a generous application of lipstick with thick eyeliner and thick lush lashes, fibres of black fallen slightly around her lower lids, a faint black smudge on her pale, shiny cheek – such thick black lashes. The colour of the lipstick is red, to match her uniform and is slightly bleeding from the edges. She has dark, thick hair, one side tucked behind her ear. (I want to say her hair is like a horse's mane, tossing as she moves her head.)

'Mind you, if you're looking for a waterproof one, then what about our *Double Fix*? It's so glossy and does a great job at lengthening. I think we have black, brown, and brownish-black in this range too.'

This onslaught of decadent detail, the minutiae of the trivial has to stop. I must say something. But I am voiceless. Snow. Even so, something is there, rising in my throat. I point a puppet-hand at one of the mascaras:

'I'll take that. That will do!'

Cathy's uniform is red. The shop is lit with bright light. There is the suave feel of opulence, of plastic, the large, too large, smoothed-out faces of perfection around me: the women in the advertisements, teeth gleaming, skin smoothed. They are two-dimensional. Without life. They are beige foundation. They have mascaraed (massacred?) eyes, long black eyelashes – thick black spiders. I must leave. Must make myself. Must get out of this shop, away from the triviality, away from Cathy, away from the red.

Cathy's expression forces control. Whatever she has seen on my face has alarmed her. I-the-puppet manage a smile, my-puppet-smile. My kind, it's okay, reassuring puppet-smile. I manage my puppet's gentler tone, its amicable collusiveness. This is what women want – to look beautiful, to be admired, to pay for this Clarins mascara to blacken their eyes and take a black eyeliner as well and to go on paying with their life.

'Oh, there are so many to choose from, it's so difficult. I'll take this one, I am sure it'll be just fine.' I hear me-the-puppet repeating in its snow-no-voice.

But the silver sides of the tall four-sided mirror are glinting, glinting in the iconographic light of glitzy advertisements. Too bright light. And something is rushing up in my throat, a geyser gushing up. Red. And the stitching of my-puppet-smile will be soaked. It is already fraying fast. My-puppet-mouth's opening. I-the-puppet catch a glimpse of myself in one of the mirrors, and see I am not just a puppet, but momentarily someone else – more than a puppet, but I don't know who... So

I remind myself again about puppets. Some other part of one's self moves them, otherwise they lie around crumpled, broken. A ventriloquist speaks for them, muffled in all their stuffing. Puppets are mute. Puppets cannot run. They cannot, they cannot... they must not... they must not...

Whatever Cathy says next has dissolved into the shiny metal of the department's mirrors all around me. Bright in the glare of the long thin light, the metal is glittering. Cold silver metal. Cold. And dangerously glittering. Something terrible and terrifying is about to come out... The puppet-master-me summons control. Clamps the puppet. Tightens the strings so tightly it cannot move. My puppet-joints are fixed, the joint nails deepen and drive in deeper, a kind of crucifixion. My-puppet-self stands there. My smile is, after all, holding up. Even after so many years, the black stitching is still strong. The joint nails are still strong. There's no sign of seepage.

Shop assistant Cathy is restored. Restored to the comfort of complicit commercialism. 'I am sure you will be very pleased with it...' I wear my stuffed-puppet-face that smiles. I have found its sutures. I am stitched together, smilingly.

Cathy has put her head down to find a bag, she can't see anything, 'I am just putting a sample in for you to try. It's a foundation, just the right colour for you...' And now she is offering me a couple of small samples. I see the white tubes in her hand, such small, exacting trivialities... 'Beginning today, as it happens, we have a special offer on skin care...'

She is pulling out something else from under the counter, a red cosmetic bag which says *Clarins* on the side... and saying, 'If you just buy one more, any one of these...' She waves a hand over the skin care range. I manage another of my-stitched-on-smiles, my puppet's snow-no-voice. 'Oh, thanks, but not for me right now. I am going away and I really only need this mascara.'

I-the-puppet pay her. The puppet-master-me tugs the strings. I jerk jointedly forward. There is a mirror in front of my puppet-self. I-the-puppet am in the mirror juddering on my strings. My puppet-master-self is determined. I-the-puppet walk, with my stitched smile judderingly out of Boots and back to my car. I am gladly, madly...

It will take a long time in the small room to understand I am also She-who-knows, and it is She-who-knows who wants to scream, a scream from time past. Red, thick black mascara, light and metal glittering in a department store have clawed it up into my throat. I don't know then, walking to my car, that She-who-knows, yes, She-who-knows has begun a different song in her strange, air-seeking sea-croak:

Five fathoms down thy father lies...

* * *

2

Looking back, I can see how exasperating it must have been. And how impossible for B or anyone else to give me the facts I believe I need to heal because my equation is wrong. The belief that facts equal peace of mind, facts equal salve of spirit is the puppet-master's mind, the organising, rationalising, being operative in the world, mind of the puppet-master who is, once again, taking control and, as always, my puppet-self goes along with it smilingly. And it is my puppet-self that draws up a form of authorisation which my father said he was happy to sign and he did so, in the small, shaky, handwriting of an eighty-seven year old man, which is also, still, unmistakably his signature. I want the doctor's records because they will tell me what happened. It will be typed on paper in black and white, in my mother's fiat form of truth. But I also want the records to help me place what I don't remember alongside the memories I still have:

– His long stride. My hand in his. Up the drive of Oldway Mansion, through the echo call of a dove and the sun-sharp lines of a blue, cool morning to the lily ponds for the fret and flick of fish.

– Waiting for me outside the school gates. His elbow bent out across the open window of the car, that orange Chrysler. A cigarette between ochre-stained fingers. In his white shirt, sunglasses.

– With his back to us. His shirt sleeves are rolled up to his elbows. The underside of his arms are a vulnerable white. He is out in the garden of our new house. We have moved to the other end of town. My mother is with me. Upstairs, she is looking down at him. 'I hope he will be happy here.' And, as she speaks, something from the dark rises. I am silenced by it.

– Downstairs. Tommy Cooper's on. His favourite. I am upstairs in my pink nightdress, as usual a sentinel, listening to gauge my mother's moods, her ragings against him. But tonight it is okay, there's the canned laughter, but his laughter is louder, warmer, and I know his shoulders will be shaking.

– A hammer in his hand, his t-shirt black and orange-striped. As he hits the windbreaker into the lawn, the hammer head comes off and catches me on my six-year-old shoulder. The tree next door has lost all its blossom and the wind is coolish and it is still too early for the wisp-ended buds of the roses.

– The pallor of his back through his white string vest, putting the electric heater in the bathroom on and he's singing 'the stars at night are big and bright deep in the heart of Texas.'

– Sitting in a chair, his broad shoulders filling it. His grey and white hair, just washed, is full and light and on the chair's arms immaculately manicured, his broad hands.

– In his pyjamas, sitting on his bed. He is weeping, saying *I can't go on like this. I can't go on...* The bed is next to the brown desolate wood of the wardrobe, its small key is glittering silver.

– In his navy anorak and cream trousers. He has his camera. Bluebell Wood. Soft sludge under my feet, dark water in mud puddles, the smell of damp earth. That particular blend of light: inviting, sinister, meeting a me that is not the me of streets and cars, but another, unknown me, seduced by the light green fronds of sunlit ferns, the green hushed gloom of trees and the poised purpled blue heads bowed by their own belled flowers. I pick a large bunch. Sometimes pulling the whole stem out so far, I see its long white root. Sometimes just roughly tearing the stem releasing the sticky salivary sap. He takes a picture. I am wearing shorts, red shorts. My hands are crammed with bluebells. Here, I am eight years old and don't know, in the vase he gives me when we get back, which I place with precarious hands on the mantelpiece, that after an hour or so, as if cursed, the bluebells will die. (Fifty years later when I look at this picture, my father will have been dead three months.) Just a picture of me – the me who will still have to learn the black letters of the word 'transience' on my sixth form page are an essay way of saying, *the blade of time.*

And the most recent memory I have, is also the last one.

– Laid out, wax-white. His mouth open.

So I imagine that when, finally, I get the records I will read an entry written by a doctor in the objectifying language of clinical knowledge exactly when my father was admitted to hospital and exactly why. I believe the implement he used will be there in the statement. I will be able to turn away and rest in the assured knowledge of the medical profession. And, with this piece of paper in my hand, I will be able to let the matter rest in black and white veracities: words on a white page.

The doctor seems to have agreed I may see the records. I am pleased and nervous. Facts. I will now know the facts. Their concrete certainties. What happened, what really happened, written at the time by the medical profession. I will know for sure whether or not he had ECT. It is bound to be on his records. And, another word holding me in uncertainty – 'lobotomy' will come clean, rush out with its arms in the air crying innocent, 'I wasn't there.' Or it will be shame-faced, staring down, mumbling incoherently, 'it's what we did, those days'... and maybe it will begin to weep at the enormity of everything it has destroyed.

I am optimistic. The certainty of fact is before me. A fish caught, flapping in the sunlight. And I, I am on the bridge about to take out the hook, letting it free. Perhaps I will even have a diagnosis: what exactly was wrong with him.

*

A grey bleakness in the sky when I park opposite the doctor's surgery. The waiting room is quite crowded. Nearly all old people. The posters in the room are gloss colours. The woman in one of them is a nurse, her cap is too white, her smile is too wide, too white; her patient is smiling, too whitely, too brightly. When my name is called, I am taken through to a small room with a table and chair in the corner. A middle-aged woman comes in to see me and I explain that I have been given permission to see my father's records. She looks anxious,
'Didn't anyone tell you?'
'What?'
'Well, your mother has refused permission.'
'What do you mean, she has refused permission?'
The woman's eyes tell me she is weighing me up carefully.

'If the doctor hasn't got anyone with him, I'll go and ask him. See if I can clarify things...'
As she leaves I bring my fists down hard on the table in front of me. I have never, ever felt so angry.
She is quickly back.
'The doctor says he phoned your parents' home and spoke to your mother. She wouldn't give permission for the records to be released. The doctor says he will call you. Perhaps your mother was protecting you?'

The doctor phones me. He had spoken to my mother who had tried to stop me. He doesn't reveal what she said. However, now that I am insisting and my father has agreed, he has to make sure that I will not be disturbed by anything that might be in the records. He needs assurance about my own mental health. I explain all this to B who agrees to write him a letter, and she does, pointing out that I will be helped to understand myself if I can see the records, and am strong enough, given her support, to deal with whatever is in them.

I return to the surgery a week or so later and, after another long wait, another, younger, secretary appears. I am given my father's records. She suggests she will photocopy them and let me take my own copies away. I leave clutching an official manila envelope and I am very nervous. My car is parked under a chestnut tree in the car park. I sit in the car, barely aware of the brown curl of the leaves beginning to fall, and ease the wad of papers out, beginning, as quickly as possible, to read through the records to find the facts I want. The statements that will tell me what happened, the exact date, the exact implement, the exact reason for it all, and the exact treatment. I will have the facts. I will have it all there: the cold of the unalterable, frozen there. Ice in the blood. And now I, too, will say, perhaps even to my mother: 'look, you see, no matter what you say, no matter what you've told me, it's written here. Here, all of it's here, in black and white.'

But the need for the letters, with the denouement I want, is a story I have created. A fiction with a fairy tale ending a – well, we will all live happily ever after now that we have the facts. That peace of mind ending has the authority of sunlight. An ending of brightness. Except that I have made it up.

The records surprise me. They are letters. They are properly headed, addresses both sides and the crest of the hospitals stamped on the top. The hospital name and address on one side, the GP's name on the other. I read the doctor's address and I am taken back to her surgery. Back then, in 1965, they wrote letters. Letters from the registrar to my father's GP, written in complete sentences. And, as I am quickly beginning to realise, they are incomplete. The first letter is April 1965 and they are in date order; the last letter is November 1970.

They describe my father's bland, nervous smile. His weeping, when he thinks everything has gone wrong. The registrar, a Mr Dare, writes: *He will do himself great harm if he goes back to work.* They record that the consultancy firm he worked for dismissed him and took back the firm's car after he had been in hospital a couple of months. They mention, later, the job he manages to get with Securicor. And a bit later, it is recorded he didn't last long with Securicor. Clearing some of his things after he has died, I find a picture of him in his Securicor uniform, looking very handsome.

I show the picture to B. She agrees. I tell her what I remember:

... the brown polished truncheon he had with its ridged handle and brown leather wrist thong. Its weight in my hand...

Though it's the first letter that is the most disturbing. It says my father was discharged, two days earlier, from St Francis Hospital. The rest, written in small typeface, shocks me:

This is just to inform you that your patient was discharged from here on 13th April 1965 with a diagnosis of probable schizophrenia.

I have taken the letters in to show B, telling her about the first one before I give her them. B says exactly the right thing:

Schizophrenia... it's a frightening word isn't it?

Yes, I was terrified when I read it.

But I want to point out that it says 'probable'. 'Probable schizophrenia'. I want to say, *but B, don't you see, it's not definite. Only 'probable'.* The uncertainty unnerves me. I-the-puppet-master am not satisfied. This will not do. Was he, or wasn't he, schizophrenic? How can they possibly write: 'probable'? I want certainty.

And, although I am very slow to see this – I must have read them several times – nothing that happened before April has been given to me. I still don't know anything about his emergency admission to hospital, the event, the implement – nothing at all. I contact the doctor again for the earlier records. Nothing else seems to have been kept. Certainly they aren't on my father's file. The doctor insists: 'You have been given everything we have here and I doubt there is anything kept anywhere else.'

Were they of interest? I ask when B returns the letters to me in our next session.

Only as far as they pertain to you.

Unsatisfied, my consuming desire for certainty converts, as if it matters at all, into a question – I do, after all, have some dates – what day of the week was April 13th 1965? At home, I google the question and very quickly have an answer:

1965 *U.S.A. River Flooding Tuesday 13th April 1965: The Midwest continued its problem weather after a large number of tornadoes on Palm Sunday rivers are now at flood conditions along the Mississippi affecting Illinois, Wisconsin, Minnesota, Iowa and North Dakota with mass evacuations and already a number of deaths caused by the flooding.*

A Tuesday. The day my father returned from hospital was a Tuesday. Tuesday 13th April 1965. Am I overjoyed? I don't know, but feel I must have been as I write now. Am I already at home when he comes in? Am I sitting in our back room with the red carpet and the French doors having my tea? Baked beans mushed into sauce, fish fingers and dippy tomato ketchup? Am I watching television? A cartoon? Scoobie Doo? Fred Flintstone? Perhaps the radio's playing? Are the Beatles singing? *I wanna hold your hand?* Or The –Dave Clark Five,

Bits and Pieces? I feel sure the BBC news will not have reported the flooding in the Midwest. It would have been too far away those days to be reported, wouldn't it? But I know it was a Tuesday he was discharged. Am I more puppet, less puppet-master? I don't know. But I am singing, 'Tuesday, a Tuesday!' I have, at last, a fact.

But She, She-who-knows, is silent. Yes, a Tuesday. My father returned on the Tuesday of the Midwest flood. But She knows he returned to shore with water in his lungs. She knows he was still a drowning man.

*

It takes me a long time – too long to really understand how therapy works. A very long time to relax enough to let my mind go like a bee from one flower to the next, wheresoever, as it wants, and to allow B to make an incision into the feeling life, to pull from the very small, often trivial story, the emotion that may be lurking there. I know I must be as transparent as possible, of course I must, but sometimes I can't accommodate a thought, B's thought, about whatever it is I am talking about. Sometimes her remarks seem so far from where I am, I can't understand why she says what she says. One day, we are talking about my mother, trying, as usual, to get to what the difficulties are. I am hesitant:

I can't share things with her...

What kind of things?

And whilst there are indeed many things I could say, some would be a repeat, and some wouldn't take us very far, so, following the whatever comes to mind principle, I say:

Well, I might say to her something like 'I think it would be good to keep bees.' And immediately, my mother would dampen the idea. Crush it somehow, crush it with her matter of factness. Her 'all that would be too much like hard work' attitude. Said in her fiat voice. And really all I would have wanted to tell my mother was something more important. Tell her about the beauty of a film I'd seen where the man keeps bees.

What is important about this film?

Well... and now I know I can't say what exactly is important about this film and why it has suddenly come, at this point in our session, to mind. I try again.

There's this man, he has bees and it's such a beautiful film...

B interjects:

So perhaps you were getting lost in the idea of a rural idyll. Idealising things?

I am unable to speak. I don't really understand why I can't say any more. I don't know what to do with B's question. I want her to understand how much I want my mother to appreciate the things I enjoy, the things I think beautiful. Or at least I believe this is why I am struggling to tell B about how my mother can be so crushing. But I will know later; though it will take me a good while longer to understand it, there is another reason why the film about bees has come to mind and it isn't really about bees at all.

As I much as I wanted to share my sense of the beautiful with my mother, I couldn't. Just as I couldn't make sense of what she told me when I was a child, or even later. My mother simply had her story. My heart was quicker when she spoke, fear dry in the back of my mouth. Her fury and hatred of my father was embroidered in all the words; her own bewilderment, her own sense of betrayal too. What happened, according to my mother, was a sudden eruption of their perfect marriage, their fourteen years of happiness. Her voice wistful, she is saying once again,

'Your Dad was blonde when I met him, you wouldn't believe that, of course...'

I didn't. My father's hair was always black and later greying. 'I didn't know you had such a distinguished looking man as your father...' my sixth form English teacher says after a parents' evening. And I am proud. My Dad *is* handsome. Very handsome. Everyone says so.

'...but he was blonde and tanned. All that sun and salt air from working on the boats. He took tours around the bay. First time I saw him... walking along one day in jeans, long lovely slim legs...'

My mother's stories compel and repel me. As a child and as an adult too. Always she says the same things, always she adds something else. I listen, always hopeful for something that will be clear, ground me, enable me to know what happened, what really happened.

'And I thought I would have my ol' Les back... Les, lovely legs, that's what I used to call him. I thought he would come back, be like he was... but he wasn't normal. All he wanted were his books and his fags and he would sit by himself while we were all in the dining room. He didn't want to talk or play with any of you three children at all. We had been so happy until then, but after he came back from hospital I always thought it was as if he was in a glass cage. You could see him, but not touch him, and he couldn't break out... He'd hit his head. That's what started it... we were just driving out to some friends. They were having a party. And we went up Cudham Lane...'

And now my mother is almost crying,

'I couldn't bear it when I saw him behind bars. He was looking out and the window had bars. I hated leaving him behind bars.'

Somehow, some way along the way, I have learnt not to ask anything. Perhaps because she was so upset and I too afraid about what happened back then. Perhaps because her moods could change so quickly, her anger rise or her silence. Perhaps because I remembered other things:

– My father is slightly stooped and he is wheeling a bike towards me. Turquoise. A shiny dark sea-green turquoise. Three gears, a fat hub on the back wheel and cream tyres. The saddle broad and cream and behind it there's a large saddle bag on a small rack. The sloping bar down the middle says Gemini 22. Not the scratched second hand red with the mean black tyres of my other one. Brand new beautiful. I am silent and unable to move in disbelief. But no, it *is* for me... 'and the gears change like this...' He puts his hand on the handlebars, as if to move the proud silver lever, 'but you are supposed to pedal backwards...'

And I am allowed out on it alone. I am ten years old. And now I am not thinking of my father – I have just seen the musical *Oliver* and it's early summer and there is the scent of roses in the air and the sky is blue and I am cycling up Tubbenden Drive and singing as if I am Oliver, throwing open windows, *Who will buy this wonderful morning, such a sky you never did see?...* and I am also the cockney flower girl, *Who will buy my sweet red row-ses?...* wanting *not to know of,* pedalling round and round and round, furiously, further and further away towards – *who will buy my sweet red row-ses?* – the *not ever to be known of...*

Perhaps, though, I didn't ask because, most of all, I wanted my father to be okay, to be a good man, and maybe somewhere I felt he was something else, so I couldn't say to my mother what was in my mind. *Did he murder someone? Mummy, did he go to prison? What actually happened?*

Inevitably then, my mother's story about what happened became my story. I had no other compass. No other stars for navigation. And always I listened, desperate to hear anything new. And, as she said, 'I can talk to you', her story, with all its inconsistencies, discrepancies, and consistencies was one she kept telling and re-telling me:

'... We'd been invited to a party, that was the Monday, some friends of his in Sevenoaks, work people, and well, he wanted to go down Cudham Lane, but the weather was bad. And after a while he decided that maybe it wasn't a good idea to carry on. So he started to back the car round into one of the small side lanes and began to reverse down it. But it was difficult to see out the back window. So he opened his door, you know like he does sometimes...' (and I did, his head turning, looking back behind him, the door swinging, car shunting backwards, and an assurance, a control, a skill I don't think he had with anything else) 'and, well, it was hard for him to see where he was going and I guess he was in a bit of a sweat because he wanted to get to the party and the car slipped. The weather was really quite bad and everything and the car seemed to slip and somehow he hit his head on the door. It must have been quite a knock, because when we got to the party they joked with him. "Your wife been knocking you around, has she?"... You see there was quite a bit of blood. He had to go and wipe it off. Well, that was on the Monday and then on the Thursday we had to drive to that work dinner in Soho and he said to me, "You'll have to drive home. I don't know the way," and then he woke up on the Saturday morning and went downstairs... We had been so happy until then... You remember Cudham Lane, don't you? '

*

In all the time I have been going to B's, I have only ever seen one other person at the house. Timing is usually well taken care of. About ten minutes at least between clients, or patients – these words are awkward, they don't fit, and to use the most formal, analysands, seems archaic. But whatever word you might use for the troubled people making their way to a therapist's, the necessity of the enterprise rests to a large extent on their suspension of disbelief: they alone are the therapist's sole interest. The woman leaving the house is large, her round collar-framed face red and, as the door shuts back, back to its bold no-admission-yet behind her, the words of the room and the self are to be gathered. So she stands on the top step, gathering. Watching from my car, my heart too gathering for her. I, too, know this need for gathering. Hers, a grey-coated gath, gath, gathering. Her buttons done-up to the neck, clink, out of the black metal gate and now, when she steps into Brow Road, her sobbing is silent.

By then, the beginning of winter, frost on the pavements, I am feeling my therapy is going nowhere. I can't get B to understand. She just doesn't understand. I question her experience, I question her qualifications. It is the first time I let her see I am angry, really angry.

Have you ever treated anyone with psychosis before? I don't wait for an answer. *I've heard... and read* (extra emphasis to make my case) *that it's neurotics only who can be treated with therapy. It doesn't work with psychotics...*

B doesn't rise to my challenge. But quietly lets me know that she knows what she is doing and tells me what I am saying is:

Very NHS thinking...

And I know that she is once again reminding me there are different models for treating mental health. And it is very important to say B never calls me psychotic. She talks helpfully, repeatedly, only of the psychotic part of the mind. The part that is like dreams. B knows that the mind, the self if you like, can split into bewildering parts. How often she tries to help me see these different parts of the self. And when I am finding myself and my responses inexplicable, she is confidently there to remind me, *this is a very young part of you.* In the hospital, of course, she knows I was truly horrified, truly bewildered that no-one used the word *psychosis,* that no-one ever helped me to understand what had happened to my mind. That I was given no chance to explore that recurrent thought: my father tried to kill himself and I think I saw a lot of blood. I was given tablets, white tablets, each evening which I was told to keep taking for a while after I came out of hospital. And, whilst both of us in that small room could see the efficacy of this to calm me down, both of us knew, in our own ways, they were never going to really help me. I was very cheered when, early on in our work together, B expressed this view.

Tablets only work for a short time... to get really better, you have to look at what's in your own mind...

But now I am bloody-minded, feeling patronised and, underneath, losing hope that, since everything was still so painful and since I was having two-year-old tantrums at home, I would ever be well again.

It's all very well for you... this is just your job. But this is my life!

If I had been lying on the couch, I wouldn't have seen B's reaction. But I am sitting opposite her. She starts, her eyes blink hard, and I see her jaw stiffen in her cheek. Immediately, I feel both dreadful and proud of myself. I replayed my words over and over again. I was proud of myself, I had risked being angry with her.

Just your job... but my life... my life!

By the next session I was wretched about being so angry and said so. B accepts me back with grace and professionalism:

I don't want just good boys and girls in here.

And in saying this, I see she really means she doesn't want puppet-masters and puppets. B wants She-who-knows. She-who-knows and who has always known what it is to be angry, really violently angry. B has already seen this She. When I swore at her over and over again, just before I went to the hospital a second time. Although I-the-puppet under the puppet-master's sway cannot remember this at all.

*

The walk up from the station becomes, eventually, familiar and pleasant. And Brow Road itself, pleasant too. Tree-lined, long and somehow welcoming. I use the parking meters to check the time of my appointment. A small open-backed lorry parked at an angle in the middle of the road clunks down at the back. There always seem to be builders and scaffolding in Brow Road, hollow clanking poles echoing, the voices of the men in tilted caps, orange vest tops, a logo. How much I like B opening the door. But before that, there's the black wrought iron gate, slightly stiff, and the pots of various plants. Today some new purple star ones, white in the centre. In the front garden a soft pink flowering bush. I like its delicacy. Yes, the walk to and from Brow Road becomes familiar and pleasant, though my father, the *pater familias,* with each step, increasingly unfamiliar.

Though I have learnt by now, really know, B doesn't want dictionary definitions, she doesn't want commanding controlling puppet-masters. Nor does she want collusive or compliant puppets. She says it in her way, and in different ways, over and over, because I am such a good puppet and, because I am so good at being a puppet-master. So today I don't want to let her feel that dictionary definitions are all I have to offer. I want her to know that I want to engage seriously with her, with myself.

You know, my breakdown, well, it was also about language... Words weren't working for me anymore... Woolf talked about the railway line of a sentence didn't she? Wanting to escape it? Something like that... I had a block, a question of form, the suffocating lyric self, the poetic, lyric self, the 'I' that ranges everywhere, through everything, the culmination to conclusion...

B is listening.

... and I couldn't go on repeating the same, the same shape in the same form, the thinking stuck, me stuck... I'd been given some Wittgenstein, I wanted to read more – and when I was teaching, I had no time, I was always, always focused on the children. The new head made it worse. Only ever focused on the children. Didn't he realise that staff need to refresh, re-think, revise, grow? A few years ago Francis bought me 'Philosophical Investigations' for Christmas. I spent the whole day reading it... changed my thinking... And so after I came out of hospital the first book I read was Wittgenstein's 'On Certainty'.

Why that particular book?

She-who-knows would explain, if she could, that it is a question of language. She knows, as B does, that I-the-puppet am pre-occupied by the problems of language. And, by now, you know too, I-the-puppet master loves words, looking them up in dictionaries, searching out and checking all those words which I think I know the meaning of and using them, some correctly, some not. Always a surprise to have used a word, found out on looking it up that it's not what was meant at all. Perhaps our need for etymologies arises when we are insecure. Certainly insecure, the puppet and the puppet-master both need the securities of words.

She-who-knows thinks differently: take adjectives, with their hooped-round-the-waist way of holding the world in. Or adverbs. Consider their dictatorial manner. Their exclusivity. She held the book *tightly*. Ah, so now we know! We know this *is* how the book was held. We know. And then there are nouns – nouns, slung out and dropped down. The world anchored on the sea-bed of nouns.

But down there, too, is all the stuff that bubbles away unspoken where She-who-knows is. How will She-who-knows describe the thought which, as B would point out, comes, mostly, after all, from somewhere else? That place where, for me at least, words don't seem to be. In the room, the light is darkening. Why that book? *On*

Certainty? I-the-puppet don't seem to know. I don't have words. I don't have my own words. My thoughts float:

— a hospital bed, an antiseptic-steamed-dinners smell, the nurse's box-flap white hat, heels in Lino: small, squidgy, light-shifting dents, metal tube frame bed railings, yucky green, pyjamas, stripes, blue and white, pillows, a yellow face, his face, yell- yell-

'He was the colour of the wallpaper in the hall...' my mother is saying. Twenty, thirty, forty years on and still the story goes round. It's woven into my mother's house, the piles of clothes, the old photographs, the cupboards stacked with bric-a-brac. The story woven into her house is the same one woven into me too, wrapped round and round in that long swathe. 'The drugs gave him jaundice...' And I know this to be true, I remember it and it's there, too, in the letters. '... He hit his head, you know. We were driving out to some friends. They were having a party. And we went up Cudham Lane. Surely, you remember Cudham Lane? The weather was so bad – everywhere was slippery...'

And I do. Long. A mile or more and a first boyfriend, his mini parked off the road, in a lay-by in the dark. Passing headlights, lighting on us for a few startled seconds. And before that, a walk with the girl guides learning to cross the road when we came to a bend, but otherwise to walk in the direction of the on-coming traffic. The guide leader's face rubicund with dry no-nonsense skin, brown eyes. Her flat, so sensible brown lace-up walking shoes. Her press on, press on manner. Standing in the middle of the road waving us all across. And the lane winding on, the small offshoots, tracks leading to stiles or gates and the fields and the green. The greens. So many different shades of green, making my being jump. But I am baffled at the one shade on the powder paint tin. GREEN. And only one blue for the sky. ('But don't you see, it's lighter here, where the blue pales to an airy white? And there's that single long cloud...') Yes, Cudham Lane: the guilty flashing headlamps, an aeroplane humming in the summer sky, walking in lines, the warm zinging pleasure from the rhythms of my own body. All those greens.

'Well, your Dad and I had gone out for the evening. It was a work do and your Dad hit his head on the car as he was reversing...' my mum is saying. 'We ate well that evening, we were in Soho... I had that dish with fruit and cream and meringue, lots of cream. Funny what you remember, isn't it? I had never had it before... only just learnt the name Baked Alaska, that was it... your Dad had steak, well, you know, I never buy steak, it's too expensive and it isn't particularly good for you, and it didn't agree with your Dad. I wondered if that's what affected him that night... He had this row, you see, with someone who said, "And you're out!" Well, your Dad put on his coat, you

know, that dark overcoat he had, and said to me, "You'll have to drive home, May. I can't remember the way."
"Oh, don't be so silly, you drove here!"
"No, May, you'll have to drive". So I did. All the way home, he kept on saying,
"Promise you won't leave me. Promise you won't leave me."
Then this liquid came out of his ear. It was on the pillow the next morning, and you know, it's a funny thing to say, but your father never smelt the same again after that. Then on the Saturday morning, he went downstairs and... I got a towel, put it against his neck and phoned for an ambulance. Then I took the three of you over the road to Mr and Mrs Jolton. He was a colonel back from India. She was a nurse. It was very nice of them. They looked after you while I went to the hospital with your dad. He was in hospital for twelve solid months. I used to go every day to see him and took the three of you at the weekends. I always thought that was important. But one day he discharged himself, came home, took the car, the little money he had, his passport and ran off. You three children were all in school. I phoned the bank and they said all the money had gone from the account. I phoned the hospital too. They said there was nothing they could do. He drove to Dover... only came back because he didn't have enough money, I suppose... he wanted to go to Europe... but all that was a long time ago now...'

'And, Mum...' I am so much older now and have begun, thanks to B, to dare to ask, desperate to know.
'Do you think it was for attention? Or that he meant to kill himself?'
And now she says something she has never said to me before.
'Oh, no it wasn't for attention,' she shakes her head. 'I would say it was hallucination... voices were telling him to do it...'
'Did he ever say anything about it to you? '
'Oh no, your dad didn't talk...'

And it's true he didn't. Nor did my brother or sister, at least not with me. My brother was two and a half that Saturday morning in 1965. Once he did tell me about the railway bridge. In hospital, my father made a fruit bowl, a little wooden stool and that railway bridge. It had sponges painted green for bushes on the sides. For my brother's train set. My sister was four years older and we didn't share our worlds. My mother was the only one who told her tale, Ancient Mariner-like. And I suppose, when she did, there was no room for my brother or sister to speak either. Maybe they did say things when I wasn't there to hear or I was, but I don't know. Though, I am sure of it now, somewhere we knew. Even though silence seeped through everything, we all knew there was an event. And there was a thin white scar on my father's neck. Visible in the tanned folds. I asked him about it once because I wanted to know. To know something that I didn't know I knew. I wanted him to say. To put it into words. I wanted him to find the words to let me know that what I knew deep down wasn't just nouns drifting around on the seabed. I wanted a vocabulary, I wanted a language. His vocabulary, his language. Not my mother's story. His story. I wanted *his* story. I wanted him to say what happened. What *really* happened. And I wanted him to find the words to re-assure me, that he was okay now.

But he couldn't and he didn't, because he wasn't.

He muttered something about an accident as a child, though I knew this was a portcullis coming down. He'd come back from work, *I have got a splitting headache, like a knife going in...* The psychiatric consultant, a Mr Birley, says the same thing in one of the doctor's letters: *his chief complaint is of a headache.* And, instead of words, or any kind of talking, my father took drugs (anti -psychotic ones, the same ones, unreviewed for over fifty years. Mr Birley's letters say this as well: *I think he should stay on Stelazine indefinitely*). And my father had a black scarf. A black scarf with silver lines running down it. And if it wasn't wrapped around my father's head, it would hang from a drawer in the blank wood dresser – creased, frayed, lifeless.

So he didn't talk, but most afternoons he did sleep. And, as if to find some kind of salve in sleep, to shut out the day, my father would blind himself with his black scarf. Whenever I got back from school, anxious, and peered into his room, I'd see the scarf's shaggy knot at the side of his head. The years of his drugged silence, and the years of desperation – his, mine, all of ours – knotted there. And I wanted so much to speak to him: wake up, Daddy... I don't understand why you are not at work, why your head hurts... why you have to sleep... and Daddy, I don't have your story... I don't have... I don't have your words, and Daddy, don't you realise I'm going under... and I... I can't see your eyes, I can't see your eyes... Daddy, don't you know I'm drowning too... And O my beloved, the water's so dark.

*

There are times when, going to Brow Road, I am more relaxed. I look at B more easily, smile, perhaps, consider what she is wearing. She is petite, slim. I am tall, broad with long arms, long legs. Nothing I would wear would suit her or vice versa. Most of all, I like a warm, plain green dress she has. It brings out the colour of her eyes, compliments her dark hair. She looks elegant, is elegant. And is that another reason why I don't want to lie on the couch? I like the colours she chooses. I like looking at her.

Tuesday's session I have a piece of writing with me. I draw it out and – this is also a sign of my growing trust – instead of giving it to B to read silently, I read it aloud to her:

'We love the oysters: scallop-shaped wafers filled with marshmallow and (thicketylicketylippety) ice cream. The van, in the vibrating mirage of blue-fumed heat, is shimmering pink and vanilla. And the mixer is whirring and a wafer is opening and the pulled-down handle is creamed coldness whirling. And in the sprint, in the four o'clock satchel-swung sun, the pavement is blunter, the tarmac softer and the girls, in blue-striped dresses, sandals and straw boaters, are a queue of classroom faces, but paler.

Across the road is my father in his orange Chrysler. He is waving. And, in all this sunlit brilliance, my father's shirt billowing in the breeze is clean crisp-cuffed white. And his hand is tanned. And he is wearing sunglasses. And his watch is a metallic glint. And he could be, I realise now, a Hopper painting (bright and, in this sunlit brilliance, lonely). And he is waving, looking in the mirror and waving again, come on, hurry! I've come to take you home, are the words in the pleased of his shirt and the pleased of his watch and the fine, handsome pleased of his dark hair and his tanned hand waving not to any of the others, just to me. And I am the princess who is to be pleased: chauffeur-driven. I open the car door, fear in my accusatory: 'why aren't you at work?'

And B, for her part, always thinking, questioning, trying to help me find the words, knows, even though I have read this aloud, I am stuttering around other silences.

This seems a very obvious Oedipal thing to me, but perhaps you are hinting here, at the end, there are things that are very difficult to say...

And so the work in this small room goes on. In the struggle for words, in the struggle to remember, in the face of what B calls *that which cannot be thought about.* I sometimes refer to paintings, an image sometimes coming to mind, but I can't always put words around it. Picasso's weeping woman was one. But even when B says:

Well, why do you think you have thought of this picture?

Why have I? I can't say. It will be later, much later, when I will know it is because Picasso's *Weeping Woman* is fractured, broken; she is crying; she is screaming. I simply say:

I like the disruption of realism in Picasso. I like analytic cubism... I like images of all sorts, all their colours.

It is not often I say something positive about myself. B comments immediately since she is much more aware of my self-hatred. She tackles me about it:

You keep putting yourself down, attacking yourself really, but your appreciation of art, it's a gift... Are you going to stop doing it?

The question rests between us.

You know images might even help...

I don't respond, but do begin to look out paintings and pictures, use them to help me find words and, as B is trying all the time to help me discover, feelings too.

*

This image is moving. YouTube, black and white. The Eurovision Song Contest. It's 1967. Nearly fifty years ago. Sandie Shaw singing. Imagine it or check it out – her hair long, page-boy, falls over her face. Her dress, very short, with sequinned netting. She is pretty. A girlish look in her eyes, in the way she throws her head back. Her eyes have black liner. Her eyelashes are black, thick black. What do we, those two seven-year-olds who have stayed up so late think about her? The pumpy, jumpy, glittery, tinkling music? The clean clarity of her voice? The spinning carousel mirror in the background? Her very short dress? Her face? The words she sings? Do we think she is a woman dressed as a five-year-old in her best party dress, with thick black spider eyes?

These fifty years on, sitting at my AirMac, to my surprise I see that one of the backing singers is wearing sun glasses and around Sandie Shaw's throat is a choker, flowers – glittering.

And while watching Sandie Shaw, I realise I have forgotten to mention something to B, something very important about my stay in hospital. After six or seven days in the psychiatric ward I am, for a short time, permitted to leave the colourless, dull lino floors, the blank walls, the showers that made you think not of water, but gas coming out, all the crying, all the bluntness. I am allowed out.

Outside, April is swanking in sunlight. And there, just beyond the car park, as I walk towards the road – in the surprise of, in the seeing of, in the pale froth of, in the shrunk to a noun of, for the naming of, but still in the jubilation at the glory of – are trees, pink-clustered, newly petalled cherry blossoms!

*

And, eventually, session after many more sessions, I begin to talk more easily:

You see, my dad would be in when I got home, but he would be in bed. The curtains would be closed and he would have tied a scarf, this black scarf... with a silver line running through... round his eyes to shut out the light. He would be back from work early, too early. Everyone else who worked in our street were commuters; they would walk back, brief cases, umbrellas, hat, home from the station around six or seven perhaps... my dad would already be home and he would say he had finished for the day, but I knew he hadn't... or he would say he had a blinding headache... and he would take aspirins, lots and lots of them. I worried about his stomach... suppose... I was old enough by then to know it was very bad for your stomach. I thought he would lose his job again... and...

Now I am searching again to find words. I have reached that blank again. Imploding? Exploding? Headplode. Heartplode. Later my dictionary tells me 'explode' comes from the Latin 'explodere', meaning to drive out by clapping, to cast out. Originally, from 'plaudere': to applaud, to clap, to express approval. My grammar school education seems to rescue me too, pulls me up out of the water, tells me 'ex' and 'im' are prefixes. I think of 'plaudere' now as something in the heart or head to be applauded. Something in the heart or head to be driven out.

After this comes a third definition, this word's strange and sea-spoken secret: 'plaudere' also means 'to beat' and, of course, the dictionary is very precise and there, in even smaller letters, 'to beat, as in wings'. I have uncovered the physicality I need (and it was there in my father's sad stammering). 'Plaudere' then, is both heartplode and headplode and away, far off, gath, gath, gathering it's the flack, the sudden clap, the shamanic flight of wings. White wings.

3

My best friend, my thin friend, is walking across the quiet room, ushered to my table by the waiter at the door. Her hair has grey running through it but, after a moment, I see her simply as the same girl who, years ago, got out of the Morris Traveller. We are in the bar of the hotel at Victoria station. She still looks strong, the lithe-strong of a ballet dancer, and she still has the not-quite-sure-about-things look on her face and an easy laugh at her own absurdities. This time something about a job interview for a teaching post she has recently failed. 'Well, it was one of my answers apparently, the Head told me. Said I shouldn't have admitted I didn't know – everyone else was probably lying when they said they did, that's what he told me!' She looked at me, shrugged and we both laughed.

Reminiscing about her gap year in America, I remembered how her mother, unable to get travel insurance, cancer taking all her organs one by one, had made the trip to visit anyway. And, as the conversation drifted, I told my friend, perhaps for the first time ever, how the cherry blossom tree kept appearing in stories I tried to write.

'My mother sent me photos of it when I was in America,' my friend said. 'The tree throughout the year... gave me a record. I loved climbing the tree. I had a trapeze attached to it – that was after we'd had the rope ladder. One day I remember being upside down shimmying along a branch when the branch broke and I ended up flat on my back still holding the branch.'

'Do you still have the photos?'

'No, I don't. I suppose the photos didn't matter to me then... and, you know, now I can't remember my mother's voice... I can't remember it.'

I hear her underlying panic. Then a pause.

'I hardly remember anything,' she says. 'Thank you for remembering the tree... write it up, write it all up, give me back my childhood...'

*

In the small room, there's a box of tissues on the small table by the side of the curved wooden arm of the chair. I seldom use it. How close I come to crying sometimes and how much I don't want to cry in there. How I will wait until I am outside. But today I can't help the swallowing and the rise of tears as I speak.

I have a friend, I don't think I have talked to you about her before... we have known each other since we were four years old. She lived next-door. There was a cherry blossom tree in her garden. Her mother... her mother worked in the path lab, looking for cancer, you know, signs of it in blood. She had wanted to be a doctor, but she was a girl; Wales, she was born in Wales, a coal-miner's daughter... and, well, I met my friend again... last Friday I think it was... in the Victoria Hotel and she told me her mother took pictures of the cherry blossom tree through the year and sent them out to America so she could see how it was through the seasons... it makes me want to cry.

And now, I am all but crying.

But that's a very nice thing, B says, slight incomprehensibility.

I know...

— A spring wind, a cold Aprilish day, branches lilting, my bedroom window, petals, pink scatterings, everywhere, back gardens, hers and mine, just everywhere.

But here and now for these spinning, unspeakable moments, I am also in the surprise of suddenly loving my friend's mother: her jaunty, organising, common sense, pragmatic mother for this unexpected gift. I wish now, for the first time ever, she had been my mother. Not because of the days over the flat, thin transparency of glass slides, the blood, the microscope and her white coat, the closest, the closest she could possibly get to the burn of her desire, *a doctor, a doctor,* not all that, but the tree, the tree. Not the steel precision of instruments on skin, cutting at the deep snow-cold of her own cancer, but blossoming boughs. And now the close of memory: my friend's and mine, too. Shut down against the coldness of cutting, glittering silver.

*

And now it puzzles me – how I should continue telling you about all this? I-the-puppet master want to tell it all in order, in a time-unrolling-itself way with a date and a day and a consequence that goes into the next day, a 'and then I did and then that happened' and it will be all on the outside, the journey of place to place, city to shoreline, airports in between, but it isn't like that, not inside my mind, not in the mind of She-who-knows. There, She jumps, falls back, rolls over, somersaults and springs on a trampoline in mad falling air and up again lifting to a kind of ecstasy, laughing and crying and walking the high wire taut between towers as a way of seizing whatever it is to make her own sense and, doing so, She lets the puppet and the puppet-master know they are not empty hollow wood, they are not stuffed, they are not solid wood blocks, but they are zany, crazy, gyrating and angry and sad, so angry and so sad. She does this to protect and reveal, promise and withhold, point out and pass by. And she does so to show She isn't time-bound, but present, even now, moving alongside them in her own liquid vibrations – and now, right now, She is coming up for air.

Perhaps I should also add it is summer now and the weather warm and I am driving to Brow Road and I have been out of hospital the second time for about two years. Lots of people are wearing sunglasses. I cannot look at them. Heartplode, headplode. I almost rush into the room. B is there sitting on the couch ready for me.

The people outside wearing sunglasses, they're frightening me.

The sun slants hot into the room, quite often we pull the blind down. B does so now. She is calm and thoughtful and asks:

My glasses are photo sensitive, have they gone dark?

No. They're fine.

She lifts them up to look for herself as I ask:

Why am I frightened of people in sunglasses?

I don't know, but come and sit down.

The spring of the brown chair as I sit re-assures me. I pause before speaking again. Already I am feeling better.

B and the room are simple sanctuary. The world outside, the black impenetrable staring of people in sunglasses has receded. This space is quiet. Calm. Reassuring. It holds my terror.

And maybe that's why I should tell you more about Sandie Shaw, or maybe I should let you know about the buddleia, which only happened just a year or so back, or maybe describe something, years and years ago, as simple as sitting in the garden, the air subtle with rose scent and I am podding peas. Little green bullets sheathed in such a pile of pliant half-moon green casings and so few really, for all that, in the colander, and my mum making steakettes (the word 'burger' another Americanism, like 'okay' that my father would disapprove of, hadn't got to England then) and the teeth of the grater all white, moist onion and the hot lard on the browned meat is shiny, and my brother, short-haired, eighteen months younger, is kicking a ball against the back wall and the thump echoes through all the summer evenings when the sky is palely blue and airy and there is, after all, school tomorrow and the days will be secure and have their settled rhythm and they will go on like this – even though the yearn of something that might sound like *more, more* if it could be spoken and wasn't so far away and so deep under the tide of words which refuse to haunt no otherwise, the nothing else of anything other than blue summer evenings – will go on like this. Always. Like this. Like this. But they won't and they don't. And we will be, even so, as now, called in to eat.

Or perhaps I should tell you I am five or six. And the meat in the butcher's is laid out under the glass. The glass is held by silver metal frames and the glass counter is quite high and it's not easy for me to see over the top. And there are round broad red tiled steps up to the butcher's shop. They are polished, dark shiny red and I like them. And once you are up the steps into the shop you will find there is sawdust on the floor – yellow sawdust. My brother and I wait in the queue with our mother and we push the sawdust up into piles with our shoes. More of the tiles on the floor can be seen as now there are bare patches on the floor and piles of sawdust and our shoes are speckled with sawdust. And piling the sawdust to leave a shoe-swathe of bare floor is the pleasure of the butcher's. Not his clean white hat or blood-smeared apron or even the red meat with its creamy sinews or thick, fat edgings, nor the casual way he picks up the biggest piece of meat in his two, swift, skilled hands and quickly flops it down on his wood board, so the woman in front of us can get just the size of steak she wants. Nor was it the slivery liver with its inner tubings my mum sometimes got for *it's so good for you* iron, nor the big till which rung up the prices with clear black numbers for every amount, nor even the big metal hooks that hung off the rail. No, it was the sawdust, thrown, I realise now, over the floor to assuage any blood, that was the best. That, and the collecting box for the blind which stood next to the till which we could see quite clearly despite the height of the counter.

'Doesn't that man on the box look like Dad?' my brother said once. And it was true, he did. The resemblance was uncanny. We used to peer up at the collecting box each time, just to be sure that in-between visits our minds hadn't conjured another truth and we were imagining the bewitching similarity. But, no, there he was again: same forehead, same dark hair in the same style exactly, and even the mouth could have been Dad's. The only difference was that he had dark glasses on and a white stick in his hand. And somewhere in my childish imaginings slipped a knowing that this was our dad and the work he really did, meant to be kept secret since he wasn't actually sightless, was allowing his very handsome face to be photographed on all the collecting boxes for the blind.

And somewhere, perhaps in that inchoate drift between sleep and daylight sense, I thought this was why the flat wooden spatula burnt black at the end and why the fat, hard and white with small burnt pieces of mincemeat from the steakettes, lay for so long after a meal in the frying pan on the top of the oven. And why he wore that black scarf all those afternoons he slept.

*

When I begin to understand why that film about the bees had come to mind earlier, I am in Greece, staying on another island with another dovecote. Well, several actually. I love the white strut of the doves along their turrets, their white-flight dazzle in sun. I write B a letter to tease out the importance of the film.

29th September

Dear B,

Do you remember I talked to you about 'The Spirit of the Beehive'? Indeed, wanted you to watch it? You said you would catch up with it sometime...

I mentioned this film in response to my mum dismissing something about bees and you suggested I was wanting to get off on some fantasy, some idealisation of rural life...

Well, no, it wasn't that at all really. I wanted to be able to share with her the beauty and subtlety of the film, share it with you. The film is so elusive, subtle and layered: two small girls (sisters) watch a film about Frankenstein's monster which, in short, ends with the little girl in the film being killed by the monster that, at first, she seems to have befriended. The last shot of the film is the girl's father carrying his dead child through the streets. Her body is limp, lifeless, drooping limbed, like a stuffed doll. Like a puppet?

One of the sisters, Ana, the youngest one, really the main protagonist, wants to know why the monster killed the girl in the film. Her older sister, Isobel, says she will tell her later, but when she does, she creates a sense that the monster is real and alive.

Set during the Spanish civil war, Ana, nearly five years old, becomes involved, though they hardly speak, with a soldier who has hidden himself in a barn across bleached fields near their house and the railway track. Ana's mother is writing letters to someone we assume was her lover before the war. She is sending him letters. Is this the man in the barn?

Ana, still very much in her mother's unconscious, acts unconsciously as a kind of go-between and takes her father's jacket to the man in the barn. When the man in the barn is shot, his body removed to the local police station, Ana's father identifies the body and his jacket which contains his watch. Ana goes to the barn expecting to find the man, instead her father is there. Seeing him she runs away.

Although there may be many, I have one possible reading: Ana feels guilty about the watch and the jacket, but also, unconsciously, her mother's guilty secret. Perhaps she thinks it is her own father who has killed the man in the barn. She runs into the woods and can't be found. Finding herself by a small lake she sees the Frankenstein monster emerge.
Is he gentle and benevolent or violent?
The imagined world, the Frankenstein film story and the 'real' events of her life merge in elusive and allusive (the monster, symbolically, Franco and her father) ways. The pressure of the erotic, guilt, the fact of an actual and imagined murder, overwhelm her. Little Ana collapses unconscious.

I sign the letter off, but I am still in *not in the knowing of.* It is later, much later, in time future, that I begin to really comprehend why this film might have come to mind. Somewhere, at the edges, in the sessions and out of them, between waking awareness, image and dream, where the *not knowing of* and *the knowing of* are becoming the fathomful.

Could the gentle and/or violent, huge, staring, lumbering Frankenstein monster be my father? My father on that Saturday in January 1965?

And I expect you are wondering too and want to ask: what about Sandie Shaw and the buddleia, then? Well, B would say there is probably a link between these things. So perhaps I'll begin by telling you about the buddleia. I have been out of hospital the first time only a couple of months and have to go for a check-up with my doctor and this is where it starts, and it is such a seemingly small incident really, but here goes:

A long slightly winding road. Arlington Road. My doctor's practice is at the far end of it, near the library. The sun is shining, not as it does in Greece, but in that airy, big cloud way it does in England. The pavement is sunlit. The front gardens along the avenue, languid. Even the concrete post by the path, solid and blunt, in this late spring light, hopeful.

And the buddleia is in bloom – tall soft summer air-swimming buddleia. But as I walk down towards the doctor's I hear a whirring electric saw getting louder and faster, the fast-sawing, louder and louder – branches, raw, pale and splitting, wood splinters flying, purple heads flailing, falling. A glittered hacking. The man pauses, wipes his brow, then his hands. An electric cord is uncoiled out on the pavement in dumb loops and, on the pavement, the newly glimpsed underside of loved leaves, the purple flowers – drowned.

And that's all there is to it. But do, as She-who knows does, keep it in mind.

*

Today there are clouds – grey, tumbled over. B has the heater on in the room.
In my quest for facts I tell her I have been trying to find out what the Maudsley Hospital would have been like when my dad was admitted. I have ordered a book 'Scenes from Bedlam'. I want to know what it was like, the facts of his existence there.

I know he made a railway bridge for my brother. He used a green, smudgy painted sponge for the hills, and the train, a small green locomotive, would go round the tracks again and again... My brother said his earliest memory of my father in hospital was when he went up to the bed and my father had the bridge and my father looked as if he was going to give it to my brother apparently, but then he turned away again... But my brother said, 'That's for me, isn't it?' and just ran up and took it... I remember it clearly over the tracks in the front room of our house. It did have a kind of sponge on it. My father also made a fruit bowl while he was there and he made a wooden stool... We used to stand on it to look over into my neighbour's garden sometimes...

B is listening, but takes me in another direction:

Tell me how you're feeling.

I am silent. A long pause.

It's difficult... isn't it?

No-one usually asks me.

Really?

No.

Not even if something good happens? You know, how do you feel? You must be walking on air!

I don't like your railings. I have been wanting to say that for weeks.

Now there is another slight pause, then B's question:

Why's that?

They're black and they say keep out.

But even as I say this I know it isn't this, it's something else. B has her own suggestion:

I think they frighten you because they put a barrier, a very clear boundary between you and me and say we are separate.

I know why you say that... (and it's true because we both know I have difficulties with separation). B tries another tack:

Don't you think they could say protection?

They might from inside, but your other ones were a bit rotten and seemed soft.

B is smiling and says gently:

They were completely rotten, you could push your finger into them. Something had to be done.

She looks wonderful. Black skinny trousers, a grey, elegant top and a black cardigan, the colour of her hair. She has small pearl earrings. Her eyeliner is a grey, warm grey. She looks more rested than usual. I counter her remark:

But, I suppose I am naturally drawn to things that have yield...

B has her own take on this:

Softness and yield make me think of the maternal body...

And, for a while, I am happy to take this thought of hers further. We talk about a child I'd taught who had anorexia, the relationship to her mother, the early sexualisation of girls in our culture, the pressure on them to stay young, to grow up. But I still have more to say about the railings and begin again:

The railings are hard, black. And they're parallel and upright and, I suppose, I think they can hurt me. And there's something about the space between them... I think they can go into me.

Well, I chose them so they were in keeping with my neighbour's... if it's re-assuring to you...

Yes, but the other ones were kind of curly, lower.

Oh God, I hated those... So fifties.

Well, these will be much more classical... (The puppet is here now, trying to be polite since I feel I have been offensive, insulting her about the railings she has.) *They'll look good for ages...* and then I have quite a bit more to add... *they make me think of houses in London... I don't mind railings in London, perhaps because I just walk past them... Now that makes me think of Virginia Woolf, railings... Dr Bradshaw says it, doesn't he? At the end of the novel, doesn't he.... Septimus Smith killed himself didn't he?*

B nods gently, lowers her voice slightly:

Yes... he threw himself on the railings.

*

A year and a bit later and I am sitting with B, the session continuing its fragile flights and somehow the buddleia has come up in my mind.

There was this man cutting down some buddleia...

And I am trying again, trying again to... to get to the what I can't say, but still I know to try to dive down, try to retrieve it, bring it to the surface and by resuscitation, mouth to mouth, attempt to find the words.

And really that's all there is to tell you except that I tried to write a poem about it and I couldn't. The words just wouldn't unravel. So somewhere on my laptop is the stunt of a poem...

B inquires politely about the poem, but I really have nothing else to say and certainly wouldn't show her the awkward six lines that I had written. But somewhere else She-who-knows knows this somehow, amongst all the certainties and uncertainties, is the beginning of the second time. The second time I am to be taken to hospital.

Driving to my next session, I am mesmerised by the buddleia bushes along the way. I stop and park my car and am amazed to find it is next to a buddleia bush. The purple flowers taper and nod gently in the breeze. That I have parked my car by a buddleia bush seems right and fitting. I am extremely pleased by this. And I am staring at it in the *not knowing why of.* The scent is warm honey; I am in primary school again. There's the sun on the green and there are the boys I like. Today it's Roger Bennett, tall, blonde hair, and his blue eyes large and mournful. Everyone thought he was handsome. It's an easy day of playground games, *Rom pom Suzy Anna, Rom pom Suzy Anna* and my hands are in *his* and the circle of children around us are clapping and singing *Rom pom Suzy Anna* and in the corner of the playground the small swimming pool with its wood racks for our feet has seventy-five degrees written on the blackboard which hangs on the cubicle wall and there's the promise of the afternoon's cool turquoise water and somewhere else, at the same moment, in the fathomful, there's a dark room, the curtains drawn, the rounded bay windows black metal, my father lying on the bed and tied across his eyes is that scarf, with its black ragged ends. But I am in the playground and I am not, and will not be, in *the knowing of...*

Getting out of my car in Brow Road, all I see are the buddleia everywhere. I love the density of the green leaves and the purple heads, which move slowly – a slow motion at the furthest tip: exotic sea-plants under deep water. There's meaning there. I know there's meaning. Their significance is growing and I can't keep from staring, and the sense I have of them, swelling and swelling. I need to tell B about this. I need her to understand. What exactly? I don't know. But, for once, this session needs no question to begin it, no thought-through statement. I begin at once:

I was on the way to the doctor's, it was about a year ago now, last April even... and a man is standing with a long, thin electric saw in his hand by the buddleia and, as I approach, he turns the saw on and begins to chop the bush down. I press my hands to my ears at the loud thrust and hack. And even as I pass, the saw whirrs and whirrs, glittering in the sun. The whole bush becomes just a wigwam of raw, vulnerable, newly exposed, white branches. And the branches were so crudely split. And the purple flower heads had fallen and the leaves were limp. I tried to write a poem about it, but I couldn't. I just wrote a couple of lines...

And today I can't help myself, I keep staring at them. The buddleia are alive and purple and green and there are butterflies and I keep staring at buddleia, everywhere. It seems very important, meaningful... I know it has a great significance.

Where are these buddleia exactly?

In the road opposite yours and by the pub... and near the traffic lights...

I know they are everywhere and I know they have deep meaning. What I don't know is that I am anxious. Very, very anxious.

Fairly early in the next session, before we've hardly got into wherever our wanderings will take us, B says:

Oh, by the way, after you'd gone, last week, I walked around here, looking at the buddleia bushes and I thought, God, how could you have missed so many?

And before Thursday's session, Francis and I drive to a local garden centre. There is a buddleia bush there. I stare at this buddleia bush in mesmerised disbelief. A magnification of purple and leaves and butterflies. I can only just take my eyes away and we browse through the humid greenhouse plants for a while. We are both, it would seem, lack-lustre. Without the puppet-master realizing, She-who-knows is, again, beginning to call. When we get back into the car, Francis gives me a stem with a small flower already purpling on it. How did he know? How did he know to pick the buddleia? I place it between us in the car. And I cannot take my eyes away, for in the wanting of, the staring of, the *not knowing of*, the searching for, but, also, in *the knowing of* there is meaning, yes, deep significance in the eye-drawing, eye-wondering, eye-stared at purple, the purple pannicles, yes, it is all there in the mesmerics of those sun-drowsed, purple-tapering heads. As I drive away from the garden centre, I look momentarily at the sky. There's a cloud and it is with a shock I see a long thin scar of a line in the cloud which is also the long thin line I drew in my notebook just before hospital the first time.

And B says *in the next session... we will think about it in the next session...* but already it is the next session and time is slipping further back, the tightrope tauter, the somersaults higher, and maybe then I am close, too close, to remembering, and B is not well, her voice is hoarse and she keeps coughing. The next morning she calls, cancels the session. *Bless you*, I-the-puppet say, polite, concerned, thoughtful of others... *Get well soon...* And She-who-knows is seven years old and staying up late and there's a moon and the sky is darkly closing and I am with my best friend and we have our backs to the garden and there's no seeing the blossom tree and it's late, very late, and Sandie Shaw is singing...

And my father's mind is *cold and planetary* and the trees there are black and his forehead is grooved and his hands are shaking and a cigarette is fumbling as he is lighting and his tea-cup is trembling all through the tremulous years of his darkening. She-who-knows knows he is drowning. And I am four years old and I am fifty-one and... and... and I am clearing out the umbrella stand in our hall which is also the Joltons' hall and I am telling Francis not to worry and I am placing my hands on the huge slit on the back of the wooden horse in our hall and I am trying to heal the wound and I am staring at the Indian prince on the umbrella stand who is riding an elephant and I can't take my eyes away from the big single eye that is purple and lined in black in the Indian painting in the hall and I am singing and singing, but I am not thinking of my father, do not, will not, think of my father, because I am next door and next door Sandie Shaw is singing *Puppet on a String*, the UK entry for the Eurovision Song Contest, and, yes, yes, I am ecstatic, it's true really, really true – Sandie Shaw is winning!

A day later, Friday August 10th, we are going shopping at Waitrose. (This is the day after B has cancelled my session and I have cleared out the umbrella stand in our hall and I am driving, Francis next to me.) I am driving very, very slowly. As slowly as it is possible to go and still to be moving and I am staring at the road signs, and I am understanding something new and unknown and I am staring at the trees, their leaves, the beauty of their leaves, their leaves undered by the summer's breeze – pale green underwater greens, green liquefactions, green oscillations in the swell of a tidal summer breeze. I am their green and I am in the green breeze slow before storm stirrings and I am hurting with the green of their greens and it is warm and sunny and Francis is saying not knowing quite what *let's go to the park before we do our shop* and I leave the car near the roses and, sitting on the bench in the park, I watch the crows and the doves, doves nervous in their peckings, white doves, and there's... and I am staring at the roses, the red roses, just for me the roses, their reds and all for me this richness, these sweet red roses... *who will buy, who will buy... my sweet red row-ses... this wonderful morning* and I am the red plush plunder of the roses and they are all there for me and the sky is blue and the trees green and the leaves of the roses are green and serrated and my bike is sea-green and in all this green and over there a man is walking in the park and he is in sunglasses and he cannot see me; no matter, I see the black over his eyes and now black and oh how black and hurled into the sea and the soft thlack of a dove's wings as it takes off from a tree and it's the

Holy Spirit and the red arrows roaring over me all red-pointed-redness and screaming for me screaming for us all, for us all, drowning drowning and the blue water of the air tremulous and the glory surrounding me and the red red screams of blood, the red thunderous storm-jets snorting and stampeding over me, entering paining from inside but how green that water, the liquid green of the trees and in the green tidal swell as green goes black and the red jets and the summer sea-storm tremulous. I must not scream at the red jets over my head whoo, whoo, whoo...

And now coming back from the park, the puppet and puppet-master entirely gone. There's only She-who-knows thrashing around wildly. Francis knows that something is going on when he sees me in my dressing gown; when he sees my unseeing eyes; when he sees me grab the red bathroom towel as I am yelling about my awful periods, holding up the huge towel and shouting 'this much blood!' But although Francis sees She-who-knows slashing her finger across her throat again and again, he didn't know, not for sure, what was happening, because her hands were also being drawn down her face as if she was crying and he said afterwards, 'it was like a puppet show'. He didn't know that it was She surfacing from a dark sea, five fathoms down, nor that I was drowning.

So he phoned B and I just about recall that I spoke to her. But it is in the not-knowing-of that I am screaming at B, and it is She-who-knows, who knows all about rage, about dark fury, who has washed away the puppet and the puppet master. It is She who is screaming, over and over again, on the phone at B in sea-dark gutturals:

Motherfucker! Motherfucker!

Nor did I know till much later that it was B who said to Francis, *call an ambulance.* But I did know when the ambulance men were in the hall. I was leaning on the wall and my head was bowed against it and I knew that one of them was saying:
'Are you hearing voices, love?'
I was furious with the ambulance man for his patronising tone, but I did not speak, so deeply was I also in *the not knowing of* – and how in *the not knowing of,* I was down with She in the fathomful and those were folds in the scarf that were his eyes and nothing of him that doth fade but doth suffer a sea-change was there glittering and, yes, I was there too, and I must not scream.

*

When I next make way again to the small green room I am cautious, fearful B will think I am mad. Or rather, still mad. Actually, I am terrified. And I am terrified of letting her hear what I think, as this will let her know just quite how mad I am. Somehow I think she will suddenly turn from her careful listening self, drop her probing questions, stop all her creative attempts to help me open up and, instead, declare, yes, I am after all mad. And since there is nothing that can be done about it, it is unquestionably and unalterably a fact, she will jump up suddenly like the Queen in Alice in Wonderland and cry: *Off with her head.* And that will be that. But when I return that second time, after swearing at her, she is fully anticipating my anxiety and, when I try to tell her how sorry I am and how ashamed I feel, she is reassuring:

I want you to know I am sanguine about it. It was such a short time you were in hospital.
And I know you won't believe me, but there's nothing, really nothing, to feel ashamed of.

Even so, I am trembling with shame and I can still feel the fear I had in the hospital, how it was the middle of the night, how the curtain wouldn't close, how it hung half off its track, and how blunt and cold the lino was and how cold the metal frames of the window. And how the blacked-out windows opposite stared in. And there were those screams I could hear and how in all this I knew a child was dying, and, as I start to tell B,

The way my breath came was so strange... if you said I had been possessed by the Holy Spirit it would make

much more sense to me, it came in such huge gasps... like this... whoo, whoo, whoo...

And despite B's wonderful acceptance of me, I still have my arms folded, pressed tightly against my chest when I tentatively suggest,

I had a dream a day or so before hospital...

How else can I describe the experience, but as a dream? And slowly I read it out:

A hollowed out amputated foot of an elephant swirled as if on wheels centre stage. I noticed a coiled-up hoover attachment, snake-like corrugated inside it. Oh! I thought we're going there now, are we? Then my father became a warrior Indian king-like and took down a sword from the wall of our house. I remembered in the dream my mother telling me that after his suicide attempt 'they' (my parents?) were told by the doctor to remove swords my father had.

I watched/I saw/ him eye spider (I spy my little eye) slice huge bloody streaks across the 'arse' (much too beautiful to use that word), the magnificent haunches of a black stallion. I turned away. But I must have turned back again because he seemed to continue hacking until he had severed the horses' head completely from its body and the head was free floating in the air momentarily until it became a huge pantomime horse's head with thick red protruding lips (vivid like Mr Punch), large eyes, and was laughing grotesquely...

But, and I am insistent, *it wasn't like any other dream I have ever had. The grotesque laughing was to cover the pain.*

I knew I was awake as She-who-knows sang her mantic sea-song louder, and I was also dreaming. I try to convey this in-between state to B:

You see it was almost as if I was awake, and this not-quite-dream seemed particularly revelatory...

Oh, they always do! It was probably the onset of the psychosis.

B has a chirpy certainty right now, a no-nonsense, dreams are dreams-of-course tone and I am lost. Though, after a pause, committed to the enterprise, I venture:

But I think my Dad really had a sword...

B is more circumspect.

Perhaps, since your sister is coming over, you could ask her about what she remembers?

*

In the cool morning start, then the sun-streamed afternoon of early September, my sister and I are in Carluccio's, Tunbridge Wells, after a day's shopping, our ice creams melting in their glass dishes, when I finally find a quiet enough moment to ask my sister, cautiously, casual – we have never in all this time, both of us now in our fifties, spoken about what happened.

'I was wondering what do you remember about Dad going into hospital?'

My sister begins immediately. 'The coal bunker. He... Mr Jolton... wasn't he a colonel or something? His wife, she was a nurse, I think, wasn't she? And they had – and I thought that it was wicked – this elephant foot umbrella-stand with huge toenails...'
I nod to let her know I remember this too, but I am nervous, unsure how I will ask about what is concerning me most. So, thinking of the blue light flashing that can still make me jittery, I stall and ask:
'Do you remember the ambulance?'
Her reply ricochets through my body.
'No,' she says quick-fire. 'I remember the sword.'

And she remembers all sorts of other things of her childhood that she recounts quickly, the very small paddling pool we had, the wigwam she was given for a birthday, cutting her hand....

'Are you sure it was a sword?' I say, after a while, turning the long-handled spoon over and back in my ice cream bowl, not looking at her.

'It was definitely a sword. He was waving it about. I'm not a fool you know, I know what he did. Why do you want to know?'

I pause. This feels unsafe territory. I am worried she will dismiss what I am about to say. Worried that what had been slipping into my mind, unbidden, unbeckoned in the days before hospital, will be rendered a macabre imagining. But desperation to know takes over and, looking up only after the words are out,

'Well... because I think I saw a lot of blood.'

My sister's response is, once again, quick-fire, matter of fact:

'Oh, you would have.'

I don't know what my sister and I talked about after that, but when I got home, I told Francis about the conversation, the sword, took one of the few remaining anti-psychotic pills I had and went straight to bed. I slept all night and all the next day. I got up at about six in the evening, had a little to eat and then went straight back to sleep again.

Well, going to bed and sleeping, that's a very good way of processing it all... B says, when I tell her about it the next time we meet. And she adds, slowly taking it in too:

A sword... now you've really got my imagination going...

*

And, even after this, time passing in its timeless way in the small room, the desire for facts still perplexes me. I dream and wake suddenly with a discovery and can't wait to tell B:

The light, the light, the fluorescent light, it was flickering – why would I remember that?

I don't wait for her answer.

Because it happened afterwards... the light going on before my dad did what he did would not be something I would have remembered. Don't you see? Don't you see? The kitchen light must have gone on afterwards! And those kind of lights – you know, the long tubular ones – they flicker when they go on... it takes a while for them to come fully on... so they flicker a bit first... I remember it because it was safe to remember it. And they are such strong lights... so it tells me my dad wasn't in the kitchen, hadn't been in the kitchen, hadn't taken a bread knife because if he had he would have needed to put the light on first to see...

Still I want the facts, the facts, the facts and how patiently B is listening to me, listening to the detective work I am undertaking. Still I feel I am in a kind of whodunnit. Only this one is a deep sea exploration, brought about by the pieces of wreckage found blackening and broken on the yellow sands. B, however, is not impressed by my detective work, because she knows in a way I don't, that this establishing of such a fact will not, finally, help me get any closer to the feelings I am so successful and so unsuccessful at keeping at bay. She does, as on so many occasions, keep trying to move me forward, but I am stuck.

Well, we will go on thinking about it... she says in her sensible, but inviting, way.

To go on thinking about it... her way of letting me know, emotionally, I am still in *the not knowing of...*

And, outside of the sessions, next to the image of Oedipus I keep with photos on my computer, I place two more. I have found them on the web. Now, though, they are in the sequence I have created. The first is a girl with long wavy hair, her cheeks fair, her skin shining. The picture is black and white, but I imagine the girl's hair is blonde. She has blonde beautiful hair. And there is something fairytale about this girl. She would be the princess of the story. The one who evokes the queen's, her mother's, her stepmother's envy. She knows herself to be desired and, as if a spell is cast, knows, too, her own desire. She is the one who must in some way be punished for the pull she has on everyone around her. The pull, most of all, she has on her father, the King. And this is because She knows somewhere she is the wild bird of his imagination.

But in this picture this small girl's mouth, this princess's royal mouth, is a mirror image of the mouth of the King of Thebes. Black and screaming.

To understand the third computer picture you must imagine a time delay, although this image is placed, at least for now, on the same page. But something has happened and now there is a puppet-like deathliness about the figure. Is it a girl, the same girl, perhaps? A china skin of unfeeling porcelain and her neck jolts and her hair is roughly shorn, stubby and matted in places, and there are bald patches too. Her clothes are soiled. Nailed into the temples of her head are strings. To make her move. Make her a puppet.

I wonder if one day you'll say that… you care if you say you love me madly…

On YouTube Sandie Shaw is putting her head down, a pause, the music pumps, the heart's beat stopped –

And it is this song we will sing after the Eurovision Song contest. In my friend's back garden, playing in her sandpit, sliding down the orangey-red slide with its huge hoop handles at the top; the game: to grab them and let go just exactly at the point where the song reaches *Like a puppet on a* – and only after the freedom of the whoo-oosh down, when our feet hit the ground, could we, and do we, shout *string!*

So I try to tell B more about the puppet. The puppet and Sandie Shaw. I hand B a picture of Sandie Shaw in her party dress.

We were talking about having a front last week, you know, how I said my dad could put on a good front... and you said maybe I was saying something similar about myself... and, well, I was always amazed people were so taken in by my front... never saw beyond it. Saw how lost I was... This is me too.

I give B another picture of Sandie Shaw, next to which I have a put one of a puppet. The puppet has big blue eyes, a thin body, red shorts and a metal leg. There is blood at its throat.

After the session, as I walk back along Brow Road, winter again, the frost is flowering.

*

Near Brow Road is a flower shop and a Small Batch Coffee Company cafe. Today, late spring, it has hanging baskets luxuriant with white flowers. Clean against the grey walls, stark in cloud and sun. There's a card shop, the black and white cards are pegged in lines in the window. They are jokey and I have read them a thousand times when I am early. A Co-op too and, nearly always, outside is the man selling *The Big Issue,* with his white sleeping dog. And, if you turn towards Brow Road, there's a huge poster on the wall about no child being homeless. But there is also a delicatessen where I buy tandoori chicken wrapped in a white serviette, or sometimes potatoes, beans and tuna salad. In the early days, that first autumn and winter when I went with heave-heavy footfall up the hill, through rain, or grey damp, or leaves rusting along the pavements, I would buy soup after my session, usually tomato and lentil, as I walked all the way back down the hill to the station. Often there are students queuing too, having sauntered along from the college, on their phones, or their ears plugged to iPods. In summer the young women have their midriffs bare, their legs long, their skirts short. But whatever the time of year, after really difficult sessions I buy golden brown flapjacks, chewy, soft and buttery – the most delicious I have ever had. The work in the small room is hungry work. The solid corporeality of the oats, the immediately satisfying rush of sugary sweetness is much needed. Flapjack balances what happens in the room with all those free-floating, airy, go wherever you please, with whatever you bring to mind, bee-suck words. Flapjack deadens the pain.

It's Monday morning, 11.15 am, and I have taken another picture in to show B. It is from a book I am reading. A face of a young woman. I know, from reading the book, she was repeatedly gang raped as a teenager. The young woman has drawn the picture herself. The book is wonderful, all about healing, and it is so well-produced the picture appears twice: in colour as well as black and white.
This picture, the black and white one, makes me want to cry. I pass it over to B. She looks at it quickly.

So why does this upset you?

I don't know why...and I can't speak... my throat is lurching and tears are rising.

Is it because of her expression...?

Yes, I think she looks so...

Another pause and I search for the word and I feel I am about to cry... and almost before I have chosen any word at all, it has come out of my mouth...

Affronted!

B is as surprised as I am.

Well, she says, *of all the words... I never expected that one!*

And we talk about this for a while, but I begin to realise, as perhaps B does, this has not got to the unsayable thing.

The next day, I am on my way to see B again. Having spent a long time looking at it the previous evening, I have the picture of the woman from the book with me again. On my way there is a buckled metal barrier in the middle of the road near where I have paused at the traffic lights. Someone has wrapped wide red and white tape around it.

I give B the picture:

That's what it is...

I point to the woman's neck. It has a black zigzag line around it. B looks at me quizzically. So I say:

It is the same marks as on the red scarf. And on my way here, I saw this barrier and it was buckled and taped in red and white and it made me want to cry... and, if I told anyone this they would think I was mad; they would think why on earth is she crying over a bit of old metal taped by the council to let drivers know it was damaged and needed repair, wouldn't they? They would think I was mad, wouldn't they?

B is quiet, assured and re-assuring:

If it was a friend they would probably think you were a bit overwrought and they might suggest you take a break and have a cup of coffee to settle yourself.

And now, in the small room, I know that I am going to cry because this buckled barrier seems sentient and has been very injured and the red and white tape is a sad, sad, bandage and I know – and I am very surprised to be *in the knowing of* that behind this response and behind the marks on the woman's neck in the picture, in deep water drifting dark: a wound, blood, my father.

But as always the method is subtle and neither of us makes explicit what might have been in both our minds even then. Perhaps it is after that session though I say:

That thin-felt-sharpness I had across my neck in hospital the first time and for a while afterwards... well, it makes me think I saw and felt what happened... and it could explain my behaviour in the bathroom too, perhaps?

And, suddenly, I don't know what to say next ...

What comes to mind... whatever comes to mind... I still hear B saying this... and always she says without irritation or rolling her eyes in the way she does at other times when I have told her about something someone else has done and it strikes her as incredible in its stupidity, but to say so would be being judgemental.

Whatever comes to mind...

And, after a pause, as so often, I find myself saying things that surprise me or don't entirely make sense to me:

We were having breakfast a couple of weeks ago at Bill's and I had porridge and asked for some Golden Syrup. I had some last time we were there and I loved it. We used to have it at home. So the waiter brought me some in a little side dish and I tasted it, but it really didn't taste at all like the last time, nor any other time I had had it. I called him back and said, Sorry, but I don't think this is Golden Syrup... Yes it is, he replies, and he brought me the bottle it had come from. There was no reason to doubt it. The bottle had all the usual Tate and Lyle markings on it. I was baffled, but let the matter drop. Well, last week a waitress let it slip that they refill the bottles – this time she was talking about tomato ketchup. And suddenly I realised that they were re-filling the original brand with, most probably, a cheaper caterer's version...

B has a possible interpretation:

To see this psychoanalytically, it sounds like the nurturing mother not quite nurturing in some way?

I know B is trying to open things up but I also know this isn't what I am trying to say. But what am I trying to say? I don't know. Only that, whatever it is, it really matters. It is another couple of sessions before I manage to make the connection I need to the Golden Syrup episode and I can only do so because B is there ahead of me and puts the words in place for me.

By now, you see, it's not the facts per se. It's not the facts only because they are facts, the weighty certainties of explanation which as such, or so I thought, would be the bearers of redemption, the assuagers of pain. No, I am at a tidal shift, since I am beginning to understand what my mother said doesn't quite match the records.

If the records are right, well, he came home... My mother's account is wrong. He wasn't in hospital for twelve solid months. According to the letters he was an out-patient quite a long time and then had a period of three months in the Maudsley the following year. My mother says...

Poor B. I am obsessive and can't let go. My mother said, my mother said, and her terrifying accounts of how weird my dad was, how strange, how much after it all he'd changed, the bread knife, all of it still in my mind, everything I knew, *in the not knowing of* – what my mother had told me. B's next remark startles me:

Does it matter?

Perhaps B should have added the word 'now'. Does it matter now?

B, highly skilled, knows I need to separate my thoughts from my mother's to know my mind is not my mother's, her stories not mine. B has known from the outset that the rent in the swathe of material, the unravelling of threads, the whirling of the psychosis, was an opening into my own mind. And that now, as I reply, I also may be getting one step closer to its sanctity. One step nearer to the fathomful, to *the knowing of.*

Well, no I suppose not...

Though I sense this is the puppet's voice... Because I still want to say of course it matters, how can you possibly think for one moment it doesn't?

And my head is spinning. Why does it matter? Why doesn't it matter? I am sunk.

The Golden Syrup meander is, however, to my astonishment, the right track. Where the bee sucks, there suck I. I was being told one thing, but I knew something else. B is, of course, there too and suggests:

Try thinking of what happened to your father as mental illness, not seeing it all through the eyes of your mother.

This will take me another year or more. Certainly, it is a couple of years after coming out of hospital the second time, when I print out Bacon's portrait inspired by Velasquez's Pope Innocent X portrait. Bacon knows we all hunger for a story. He understands my desperate need to know: the 'brutality of fact' is his phrase for what he wanted in painting. But he doesn't mean fact in the way I did. He wasn't, to put it metaphorically, searching and searching for a kind of photographic copy; the kind of 'outside' that nowadays is recorded everywhere by CCTV camera. What he wanted to capture in his birds, dogs, grass, people, himself, was their very subjective certainties. Bacon wanted to show what it is like 'indoors', in the feeling self. I cut the portrait in half, take a picture of my father and cut this in half too, and place my father's half alongside the screaming pope.

In this way, his paintings are aligned to what B is also trying to do with me. Bacon wants to disrupt the given story, the illustrative. B wants to do something similar too. So, strangely, B's work with me is aligned to Bacon's, although Bacon's art magnifies the interior. Bacon's colour is an attempt to silence the desire for story, right at the edges. The colour is static, strong, hard, and flat. He wants to show the nervous-system-shock of feeling, and let you feel the same thing when you look at his work. B's work is gentler, the disruption much gentler, subtler, more meandering, but the given story is still, in our work together, opened to another place. The place, for me, where memory did not ordinarily, could not ordinarily, reach. Where in writing, and in the small room, the unsayable haunts. The place, perhaps, where madness taunts – both telling and silencing us. Terrifying and healing us. It is the place of violence. It is the Clarins store where, in the fluorescent shop lights at all the edges, there is red. Red ricocheting and cold silver metal glittering. But with B it is the place for finding the power to name. Crucially, it is the place for finding the words for feeling.

I take the picture I have put together of my father and the screaming pope to show B.
This picture is a new canvas of a new pain. My father's. My own.

When my dad did what he did... I ask her, my adult and child self tangled up together, *do you think it hurt him?*

Not long after this there is, to my mind at least, what I think of as a leap, a leap into language. I have a word, a word. I have a word! Indeed words! Because of course there are lots that I can muster now that enable me to heave my heart into my mouth, to think of that which could not be thought about, to say that which could not be spoken. My mother's words, her stories, were not and, of course, could not be mine.

And, you won't be surprised to know, just to be sure, really sure, I checked what was to become *my* word in the dictionary. Its definition: *to inflict a wound upon* and *to inflict an emotional wound or shock upon; to impair or damage psychologically*. I begin my session, the last one of the week, by saying:

I know this sounds obvious, a bit funny to say, but I was... well, I think the word is 'traumatised'.

'Traumatised'. Somehow it is as if it had never ever been spoken before by anyone. I feel as if I have found it entirely for myself, for the heartplode, the headplode of *my* being. 'Traumatised' is why I stared so hard at the buddleia because behind the electric saw, She-who-knows knew there was a sword and knew the electric saw was evoking it, and She also knew that my four-year-old self had the sword's thin-felt sharpness in her own body and, however much that four-year-old loved her father, it was as if he had cut her too. That I could now speak the word 'traumatised' about myself is a fruition of so much of B's work with me in the small room. A gathering.

And by the time I can say: 'traumatised,' I will have also remembered another room. The room in the house where the lawn in the back garden was surrounded by roses. The front room at number eight. Our front room: I will have remembered that room with its desk, bookcase, my brother's railway track laid out on the carpet, that painting of those African women, like Picasso's Damoiselle D'Avignon, with their heavily black-lined, staring eyes. The black metal bay windows. And, by then, though it isn't easy to separate out such young memories, I will have been able to tell B something more, and not only about the snow. By then, I-who-is-becoming is getting stronger. I-who-is-becoming remembers more and more and this begins to change my need for what I thought would be the facts. Instead I-who-is becoming – the puppet and puppet-master – and She-who-knows, relating to one another with greater ease, begin to understand what B calls the subjective certainties: the power of my own autobiography, the truth of my own imagination.

4

Imagine.

I am *wintering in a dark without window,* turning the key in the back door and sitting down in the middle of the kitchen floor, between the sink and the black boiler... the...

The frost makes a flower.

The kitchen's back door handle is shiny-smooth-slippy-hand-holdy-cold solidity. A key turned coldness. Snow-cold. Sitting on the black and white lino, I can see her outside, hear her outside. The key, clunky brassy blunt, is lying on the floor between me and the locked door and, somewhere nearby and so far off in ... the front room... *the great bay window is spawning snow and pink roses...*

My mother is out in the back garden hanging up sheets. After snow the day is sun, blue sky and roses. In our garden there are pink roses. Pink-icings with heart-yearning-soaring scents. White sheets sway, snow-blinking, snow-glinting, snow-blinding... they *step off into whiteness.* The keyhole is covered by a metal circular disc that swings up on a small brass pinhead to let in the key. The roses are opening to open centres of gold galaxies gathered, and droplets, pure domed drops, water globes, glassy-domed-darkened-watery-world-shaken-upside-down-ice-frosty pieces of snow... I can't see anything now, only her face... not the holly trees, the square wood-mossy arch, jumble of raspberry canes, rhubarb flapping elephant-ear leaves, my green swinging swing...

'Jenny, Mummy wants you to pick up the key and come and open the door.' But, Mummy, where are the refined snows of the roses? Those sweet sugaries, frost-flower intricacies, whitey-pink possibilities?

'Jen, just pick up the key for Mummy, and open the door...'

The far fields threaten... snowy sheet squares, petal-peeled-smooth-rose-scented satins, snowflakes falling dropping dark pieces... 'Come on, Jenny! Open the door for Mummy,'... rose scent soaring soundlessly... white... wordlessly white... wending a way to let me into a snow-blinding heaven....

All morning the morning has been blackening... the kitchen back door has a black metal frame. Three of the door panels are icy glass held by thin black metal.

'Jen-ny!'

Sugary-shaken-flakes, falling dark water, snowy slowly wandery white wordless wonderings... 'Get the key and unlock the door!'... The bottom panel of the door is not glass but metal. The snow drops its pieces of darkness into a snow dark mish-mashed hushed up silence... *A black amnesia of heaven.* The bottom panel black-metal-blackening... cold as snow breath...

'Get the key, do you hear me?! Jen-ny! Will you do as... *you do not do...* as you are told...' you do not do... a snow-watered-white-darkness... starless...

'Pick up that key and unlock the door!...' Blackness... 'If you don't unlock that door,' ... collateral and incompatible... fathered blackness... 'I am going to smack you!'

'But, Mummy, please don't!'

I want to please you, oh, how much I want to please you, how much I want you to know, how much, how much I like the things you give me, Mummy. Mummy, I love the dreamy flakes, the dark blue sky in my snow globe and the snow, Mummy, oh, the snow on the roses...

... and Mummy, I want you to know how much I want you to like the funny way I write... write my name and I didn't know I was so bad to write it with the spacing between the letters all wrong the 'e' round the wrong way, with the 'J' of Jenny too big on Daddy's desk, the desk by the black bay window in the front room, the desk that's got the tiny metal key with the round loop at the top, the desk and the key which are in the front room, you know the room, Mummy, don't you, the front room with the bay window, with the bookcase, those two books, 'The Spy who came in from the Cold', the purple Harper's book of poems, the room with the heavy lead pistol, with the painting of women with black lines round their eyes, thick black lines, that room, the room with the black and white carpet, with the bay window, Mummy, the great bay window... and the sword on the wall, yes, the room with all the ice glass glinting, glittering silver gold-handled-pointed cold, that room with the wild, wild-pointed-sharp-black-haired-wildness, all that glinty, glittery-blindly-metally-wildly glittering glittering... Mummy, that room! You do know which room!

The room with that great black wintered window – it was winter then, wasn't it, Mummy? There was snow, wasn't there? A far field sheet white letting me through to a heaven... starless, fatherless... that room, Mummy!
'This is the room I have never been in...'
'Yes... yes... Mummy you/I have...'
'This is the room I could never breathe in...'
'...the room with the black and white knobbly woolly prickly settee with wooden round black legs and flat round gold feet where you heard me, saw... saw me, my knees drawn right up to my chest, that's what you said, you did say that Mummy, you did... where you saw me... you did see me, didn't you... and the sword, Mummy,

and the sword, and you came down the rest of the stairs because this was the room... starless, the room *at the heart of the house* Mummy, this is the room where, in a dark without window, I was, I was too frightened to be screaming Mummy, Mummy! Wasn't I? Wasn't I, Mummy?'

'Mummy, please don't smack me!'

The dead bell.
The dead bell.
Somebody's done for.

Me? Mummy? Daddy!?!

I do not, cannot open the black metal panelled back door.

There is more than glass between the snow and the huge roses...

I do not stir.

And, so you see, even though I may use Plath at times to say... *Daddy,... black mind – whitened by a mile* of the drugs they put you on... *not daring to breathe or achoo,* I can also *say* for myself, in my own words: my gentle, kind, broad-handed, broad-shouldered, handsome, violent, mad Daddy – I always knew it was you.

*

My friend, after the recent death of her own father, is, once again, living in the house that she lived in next door all the years of our childhood. (Her mother dead for over forty years now.) My friend, who is still thin, laughs as she tells me that the junior school across the road, which we both went to, still requires the same silver and blue-striped tie as its uniform, the same blue blazer. (In the playground there is still a circle of children *Rom pom Suzy Anna*, clapping over the years. I have my hands in a boy's, *Rom pom Suzy Anna* – and now I believe I was wearing a pink skirt and can't think I ever wore a uniform at all. Can this be right? My favourite teacher is in a navy windcheater, a cool breeze billowing through it, and she's dipping the thermometer into the swimming pool.) My friend's house is number six. I will take pictures of the front bay windows before I leave. My mother will want to see them. New aluminium double glazed windows at number eight replace the black metal ones.

'We pulled the hedge down... don't you remember it?' My friend nods her head. 'There's a cine film... I expect it is here somewhere in these bookcases.' And I am smiling. The shelves when we were teenagers were full of thick purple-spined volumes about the Kings of England. Of course, my friend, I recall, read History at Durham. 'My father loved history too'... she says. 'He always felt more at home with facts...'

Now there are a few novels and other things including, somewhere, the cine films. Her father is laughing, a gap between his side teeth at the top, his dark hair flicked back when he replayed the film to us both, however many years ago that was, and I think I am in red shorts, but we can't find the film to be sure. In the back room is a wooden dining room chair. I see with delight the diamond cut on it which I only know, right then, I have always known to be there. The same chair I must have sat on without moving that cold January day, snow on the rose bushes, on the cherry blossom's branches. And even now the paint on the French windows in her house is still yellow. The handle exactly the same as in our house: hand-hold-slippy-cold. Though, as she points out, it has been re-painted a number of times. From the upstairs I look over into those two back gardens. The lawn and roses bushes have been paved. The blossom tree has gone.

I email her later about the tree. She replies with facts and uncertainties... Well, it was there in 1960 when I was born. My parents may have planted it in 1953 when they moved in, but the fact that is the same as many of the trees lining the street makes me wonder if it was planted by the builders in the 1930s. Is that possible? It became diseased, but I don't know when, though after my stepmother moved in, so post 1989. I could ask the neighbours... anyhow it had to be chopped down.

It is a May Bank Holiday Monday when I next take the train to Brow Road and its small parade of shops. I have been out of hospital now for several years. There's the sea, a blue flat distancing away, the trees are the blown-over underside of their greens, and there's light on the hoodlum crows, the fields and the light is scorching: a Van Gogh painting's there in the mad of the yellow.

I tell B about my visit to my friend's...

The holly bushes have gone, the raspberry canes, the swing too...

I remember one day her father running, swinging, jumping over the small slide, the small see-saw, monkeying over the swings and the sandpit...

The stool my father made in hospital is not by the fence, nor are any of the children at number eight peering over to see the commotion.

And I tell B the only snippet I can recall of a dream I had the night after my visit:

My father is sitting behind the windows. He looks exactly like he does in the picture I used for his funeral. He's behind the black bay windows, but he is smiling...

And although B and I will go on talking for several more years – new understandings, freer feelings still need more prismatic light and time to settle – it is in today's session, as we talk, B mentions Sylvia Plath died in the coldest winter on record. And it's today, since I have recently been re-reading my father's medical records, I show B the uncanny emblem from St Francis, the hospital my father first went to: a horse with an arrow through its throat.

The work with B has made it possible. Made it possible to dive down into the fathomful. Not because of the facts, although the retrieval of the letters helped. Helped me to see things from another way, helped me to a story that wasn't my mother's. Helped me to a story, real or imagined, but a story with me in it. One that was mine. A story for which I had had no words. Only those of my mother's. My own words silenced in my body, drowning in my blood.

And even though I have the facts about so much, including the tree, B and I will go on thinking in our next session. And, perhaps, if it falls out that way, we will talk about what has not yet been expressed in the small room:

– April, rain. On the road out the front there's blossom, cherry blossom wind-blown across wet tarmac, pale veined petals in gutters and in kerb corners gath, gath, gathered...

For now though, I clink the gate shut behind me as I step out into Brow Road. Today there is sun. New leaves are greening. Dove-call swells the air.

Acknowledgements

Thank you to my many friends who gave me such tremendous emotional and practical support during the very difficult story recounted here. From impromptu food hampers to help clearing my office; from omelettes and shepherd's pie, to chauffeuring me so readily when I had no car.

I would also like to thank my brother who stepped in with generous financial help, love and advice.

And thank you to Anna Carlisle, Belinda Giles, Andrea Hollander, Kim Lasky, Jane Mogford, Graham Powell, Nomi Rowe, and Stella Skordalellis. All of whom read the manuscript, offered thoughtful suggestions and generous praise which kept me believing in it.

And, of course, my boundless gratitude to my therapist and my partner. Both of whom plumbed some of the dark depths with me and always brought me up for air.

Attributions

All of the following reprinted with permission from Faber and Faber.

p.3, *The snow has no voice.*
in the poem 'Munich Mannequins' *from* **Ariel**, Sylvia Plath, (Faber and Faber 1965)

p.18, *not pieced, glued, and properly jointed,*
in 'The Colossus' *from* **The Colossus**, Sylvia Plath (Faber and Faber 1960)

p.31 *O gape of complete despair?*
in 'The Moon and the Yew Tree' *from* **Ariel**, Sylvia Plath, (Faber and Faber 1965)

p.39 *I simply cannot see where there is to get to...*
in 'The Moon and the Yew Tree' *from* **Ariel**, Sylvia Plath, (Faber and Faber 1965)

p.124, *cold and planetary,*
in 'The Moon and the Yew Tree' *from* **Ariel**, Sylvia Plath, (Faber and Faber 1965)

p.149, *Wintering in a dark without window,*
in the poem 'Wintering' *from* **Ariel**, Sylvia Plath, (Faber and Faber 1965)

p.149, *The frost makes a flower,*
in the poem 'Death & Co' *from* **Ariel**, Sylvia Plath, (Faber and Faber, 1965)

p.149, *the great bay-window is spawning snow and pink roses...*
in the poem 'Snow' *from* **The Collected Poems of Louis MacNeice**, Louis MacNeice (Oxford University Press, 1967)

p.149, *Step off into whiteness,*
in the poem 'Sheep in Fog' *from* **Ariel**, Sylvia Plath, (Faber and Faber,1965)

p.150, *Refined snows,*
in the poem 'Wintering' *from* **Ariel**, Sylvia Plath, (Faber and Faber 1965)

p.150, *All morning the morning has been blackening,*
in the poem 'Sheep in Fog' *from* **Ariel**, Sylvia Plath, (Faber and Faber 1965)

p.151, *you do not do...*
in the poem 'Daddy,' *from* **Ariel**, Sylvia Plath, (Faber and Faber 1965).

p.151, *A black amnesia of heaven,*
in the poem 'The Night Dances' *from* **Ariel**, Sylvia Plath, (Faber and Faber 1965)

p.152, *letting me through to a heaven…starless, fatherless,* in the poem 'Sheep in Fog' *from* **Ariel**, Sylvia Plath, (Faber and Faber 1965)

p.152, *This is the room I have never been in…this is the room I could never breathe in,*
in the poem 'Wintering' *from* **Ariel**, Sylvia Plath, (Faber and Faber 1965)

p.153, *The dead bell…somebody's done for,*
in the poem 'Death and Co' *from* **Ariel**, Sylvia Plath, (Faber and Faber 1965).

p.153, *There is more than glass between the snow and the huge roses,*
in the poem 'Snow' *from* **The Collected Poems of Louis MacNeice**, Louis MacNeice (Oxford University Press, 1967)
lines from 'Snow' by Louis MacNeice, publisher Faber and Faber

p.153, *Daddy, black mind –whitened by a mile…barely daring to breathe or achoo,*
a composite: *black mind* in the poem 'Wintering'; beginning and end in the poem 'Daddy,' *both from* **Ariel**, Sylvia Plath, (Faber and Faber 1965).